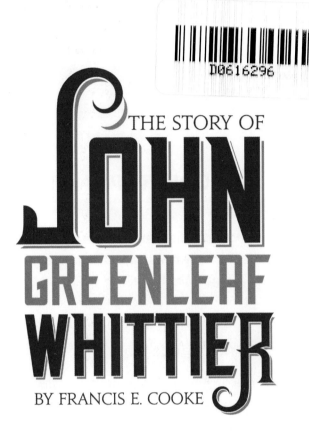

THE STORY OF JOHN GREENLEAF WHITTIER

BY FRANCIS E. COOKE

First published in 1900

This unabridged version has updated grammar and spelling.

Cover design by Elle Staples

INTRODUCTORY NOTE

John Greenleaf Whittier, the poet-philanthropist of America, was one of the heroes in stirring times, and his history, so full of incident, should interest young people: this story of his life has been written, however, chiefly with the aim of recording for them the beauty of his character. It has been truly said, "The noblest workers of the world bequeath us nothing so great as the image of themselves."

The materials for this little volume have been drawn from various American sources. I am especially indebted to *The Life and Letters of John Greenleaf Whittier* by Samuel T. Pickard.

The few poems and stray verses chosen from among the poet's writings have been introduced on account of their connection with events in his history.

F.E.C.

November 1899

Table of Contents

CHAPTER 1

THE FARM BOY OF HAVERHILL

In the year 1638, a Quaker named Thomas Whittier sailed from Southampton and crossed the ocean to America to make a new home in a strange land. Twenty miles or so from the Atlantic coast, he built the log hut which was to be his dwelling, surrounded by the woods and meadows through which the beautiful river Merrimack flows. By and by a little country town called Haverhill grew up near the pioneer Quaker's home, and Thomas Whittier helped the new settlers with advice and was held by them in great esteem. One trouble, however, he never shared with them: this was their terror of the Indians, whose ancestors had camped in the neighboring wild forestlands for centuries past, and who, therefore, looked upon the country as their own rightful possession.

No wonder it was, then, that the plumed and painted natives came to explore the settlements of the white men and with none but peaceful intentions. But when they were driven away by fire and sword, they made reprisals in the winter nights by burning lonely dwellings and tomahawking the inhabitants.

So the people of Haverhill built themselves strong places of refuge where timid persons might shelter in case of an attack upon the town, and the feeling of enmity between white settlers and Indians grew apace.

Thomas Whittier neither barred his doors nor shuttered his windows. His trust in the natives and his kind acts toward them gained their goodwill in return. They were always friendly with the peace-loving Quaker, and when he built himself, in course of time, a larger dwelling at a little distance from the log hut where he had no neighbors at hand, it mattered not to him and his family if they caught sight of swarthy faces peeping in through the latticed kitchen window after nightfall and knew that the wild men from the hills were at hand.

Generation after generation passed away, and the farmhouse descended from father to son, till early in this century a farmer named John Whittier, who was a Quaker like his English ancestor, owned the place. It was a low brown wooden building with two windows on each side of the narrow front door and three windows in the story above. This door opened into a small square entry with a steep staircase leading from it and a room on either hand. At one corner of the house, a porch led straight into the kitchen at the back of the dwelling, which was the family living place. Such a room! It was thirty feet long and had a huge fireplace at one end, round which a company of people could gather on a winter night, and children could hide away snugly in the shadowy chimney corners and fall asleep or listen to the tales their elders told by the blazing firelight.

In front of the house lay a terrace and a sloping garden separated from the steep, hilly road by a thick fence of trees and a brook that rushed merrily down its rocky channel. Across the high road stood a granary, a forge, and the barn where the cattle were housed in the winter. On the other side of the garden lay the farm and fields; while at its foot rose a steep hill called "Job's Hill," clothed with oak trees, from the summit of which a fine view was to be seen of the neighboring woods, of Lake Kenoza gleaming in the distance like a jewel, and of the river Merrimack winding through the meadows on its way to the sea. From that hilltop could be heard in stormy weather the roar of the great billows breaking on the beach many miles away.

So much for the Quaker homestead and its surroundings; now

for its inhabitants. Farmer Whittier, who was known as "Friend Whittier" in the neighborhood, was an honest, worthy man whom everyone could trust. He did each day's work diligently and seldom looked beyond it, having few thoughts or wishes that his home and daily life did not satisfy. Eight miles away at Amesbury stood a Quaker meetinghouse. Thither the farmer and his wife used to drive each Sunday in an old-fashioned chaise drawn by a steady old horse, to join in silent worship with the few "Friends" who gathered there. Sometimes "ministering Friends" used to stay at night at Friend Whittier's farmhouse and always found a hospitable welcome; but the visitors who were most often to be found there were poor travelers—tramps and wandering peddlers carrying with them packs of small wares to sell. Some of them were uncouth and ignorant people; some were sturdy knaves who demanded food rudely and did not wait to be invited to take a comfortable seat by the fireside; but the ready kindness of Abigail Whittier, the farmer's wife, and her sister Mercy flowed out to them all, and they carried with them lasting memories of the tender-hearted Quakeresses as they went on their way.

John Greenleaf Whittier, the hero of this story, was the elder son of Friend Whittier and was born on December 17, 1807. Three other children completed the family—Mary, who was a year or two older than Greenleaf, and Matthew and Elizabeth, both younger than he. It was a happy country life that the little lad led in his early childhood, playing barefooted in the summer by the brookside and making friends with the living creatures in the woods and the animals on his father's farm.

But children soon grow out of babyhood in a busy family, and working days began very early for the little Whittiers. The girls helped their mother to spin and keep the house in order; the boys had plenty to do on the farm and in the fields, where the ground was rough and stony and had to be cleared of the old trunks of the forest trees.

During the winter when the snow lay thickly on the ground, there was no work to be done out of doors for weeks together. Then, in the long evenings, the mother, sitting at her spinning wheel, used to tell the children stories of her own young days and repeat to them tales she heard from her parents of the adventures which befell the early settlers when the wild Indians with their bows and tomahawks used to come down upon the log huts and farms where the white men lived, whom they looked upon as their enemies. As they listened to her words, the young ones would creep nearer and nearer to the great open fireplace and look round timidly when the wind shook the farmhouse and rattled the latticed windows.

There was great excitement in the household sometimes, at the end of a long, heavy snowstorm, when sledges, drawn by many pairs of oxen, came slowly down the long hillside, forcing their way through the snowdrifts to clear the road from farm to farm. The loud voices of the drivers could be heard in the clear air from far away; and Friend Whittier and his boys used to hurry to the barn and bring out their oxen, ready to be harnessed to the team, while the girls prepared and carried out brimming cups of cider for the men to drink as they waited at the gate.

At times, too, when the storm had been roaring all night round the house, the children woke in the morning to find everything deep in snow; the white drifts lying against the windowpanes; the garden wall and the woodpile buried under one dazzling white cover. Then the farmer used to call out "Boys! A path!" and Greenleaf and Matthew, drawing on their thick mittens as fast as they could over their hands and pulling their caps over their ears, ran out of doors to set to work to tunnel a path through the snow from the house to the barn. They shouted merrily as they neared the end of their journey and woke up the imprisoned animals that used to look with large wondering eyes at the invaders.

The district of Haverhill was at its best in spring and summer when the meadows were full of flowers. Surely there never were anywhere else such hepaticas and anemones as were to be found beside the brook, half hidden by drooping ferns and grasses. In the woods the oaks and maples were the homes of squirrels and birds that never learned to fear the footsteps of the boys and girls, who would not for the world have done them any harm. Farmer Whittier and his family had no need to go beyond their own farm boundaries for the means of living. Their sheep and the flax grown on the fields provided material for their homespun clothes, they grew their own wheat, and the river was stocked with fish.

It was part of Greenleaf's work each day to milk the cows and carry the milk pails to his mother, who was famous in the neighborhood for the butter and cheese she made. The boys gave pet names to their favorite oxen. One was called "Buck" and another "Old Butter." If ever a holiday was given to the boys on a sultry summer afternoon, they used to drive the cattle up Job's Hill and lie under the trees resting against the patient creatures as they lay chewing the cud in the shade.

One day Old Butter, from his standpoint on Job's Hill, saw Greenleaf coming up with the well-known bag of salt, which he had been to the farm to fetch for the cattle. Down came the ox with flying leaps to meet his young master, and as the boy bent down to strew the salt, Old Butter was upon him in his headlong course. Making a great effort, the ox leaped up and just saved Greenleaf's life, lighting with a mighty blow upon the ground beyond him, happily unhurt. Kind treatment made the creatures on the Whittier's farm half human; and the young Whittiers, by making friends of the dumb animals, gained a pleasure in their early days, which any country boy might possess if he liked.

Half a mile from the homestead stood the little schoolhouse to which Greenleaf trotted by the side of his elder sister, for the first time, when a wee laddie. It was only in the winter when there was little work to be done on the farm that the children, as they grew older, could be spared. They used to trudge through the deep snow and learn to read and write at the notched and battered desks, finding it a strange experience to have the companionship of other boys and girls.

Looking back after fifty years had passed on these early school days, the poet Whittier wrote the following verses for a children's magazine called *Our Young Folks.*

IN SCHOOL DAYS
Still sits the school-house by the road,
A ragged beggar sunning;
Around it still the sumacs grow,
And blackberry vines are running.

❋ ❋ ❋ ❋

Long years ago a winter sun
Shone over it at setting;
Lit up its western window-panes,
And low eaves' icy fretting.

It touched the tangled golden curls,
And brown eyes full of grieving,
Of one who still her steps delayed
When all the school were leaving.

For near her stood the little boy
Her childish favor singled;
His cap pulled low upon a face
Where pride and shame were mingled.

Pushing with restless feet the snow,
To right and left he lingered,
As restlessly her tiny hands

The blue-checked apron fingered.
He saw her lift her eyes, he felt
Her soft hand's light caressing;
And heard the tremble of her voice,
As if a fault confessing.

"I'm sorry that I spelt the word—
I hate to go above you;
Because,"—the brown eyes lower fell—
"Because, you see, I love you!"

Still memory to a gray-haired man,
That sweet child face is showing;
Dear girl! the grasses on her grave
Have forty years been growing!

He lives to learn, in life's hard school,
How few who pass above him
Lament their triumph and his loss,
Like her—because they love him.

It was a very quiet, uneventful life that this boy led, who was to be famous in the coming years. He rarely went beyond the district of Haverhill. But he was perfectly happy whenever in summertime he could lie beneath the trees on Job's Hill, thinking his own thoughts and dreaming the sunny hours away in visions that were by and by to clothe themselves in beautiful words. Only his mother suspected this. She watched her boy with silent sympathy. Perhaps as she read the Bible to her children on Sunday evenings, and saw Greenleaf's face kindling as he listened to the grand old words, she wondered within herself whether the day would come when his name would be known in the world outside the hills that sheltered his quiet home.

CHAPTER 2

HIDDEN TREASURES

Two other members of the family living in the old farmhouse have not yet been mentioned. One of these was Friend Whittier's brother Moses, who was part owner with him of the farm. Uncle Moses knew wonderful stories of the country and country lore. He could tell his nephews and nieces all about the habits of birds and insects and the places where special wildflowers grew best. Greenleaf and he were close companions. The boy liked, when he could, to dig just beside his uncle; and, as he listened to his talk, it seemed to him that the thought of the beauty of the world around him grew clearer and clearer in his mind. Moses Whittier did not live to be old, and his sad end may be told here. One day, he went out alone to hew down a tree on the hillside. Hour after hour passed, and as he did not return, they went out from the farm to search for him. The barking of his dog drew the seekers to the spot where he lay unconscious beneath the fallen trunk. He was carried home and lived only a few days. This accident did not take place till Greenleaf was seventeen years old.

A maiden aunt named Mercy Hussey, Mrs. Whittier's sister, was also one of the family—a gentle, sweet woman with helpful, loving ways, whom Greenleaf cherished in his own home when he became a man.

In the boy Greenleaf's busy, hard-working life, there was one great want. He used to long for books. There were only about twenty volumes beside the Bible on the kitchen shelf. One of these was a copy of *The American Reader*, containing extracts from poets long since dead and forgotten. He used to pore over this reader in the evenings and read again and again the other volumes which we, who are fortunate enough to have so many more interesting books, should probably never care to glance at. He had only a little schooling in the winter months, when he learned to read and write the first steps in arithmetic. This small amount of learning wakened in him a great longing to know more; yet there seemed no hope that he could have any better education. He would probably have to work on the farm all his life as his ancestors had done.

Meanwhile, his mother guessed something of what was troubling him; and thinking it might be a comfort to him to write down some of his thoughts, as he had little chance to read those of other people, she sewed together for him a few large sheets of paper, and on these he began to keep a diary. This employment did not last long, however, and the stray verses he began to make were written, for the most part, on his slate when he had finished his sums in the winter evenings. Someone preserved the following funny little rhyme, which told his innermost wishes very truly—

> *"And must I always swing the flail,*
> *And carry back the milking pail!*
> *I want to go away to school,*
> *I do not want to be a fool."*

One day it happened that a Scotch peddler came wandering by the farmhouse on his way to a neighboring settlement, and stopped at the Whittiers' door, where, as was well-known, no stranger was ever refused a welcome. According to custom, this traveler was invited in, and he hung up his plaid and cap, laid aside his heavy pack, and enjoyed the welcome rest and food which were willingly given to him. In return for the kindness shown to him, he repeated two or three poems about his native land and then sang "Highland Mary" and "Auld Lang Syne." This was a rare experience in the Quaker home. Greenleaf stood listening in delighted surprise. It was his first introduction to modern poetry, and the verses filled the boy's thoughts for many a day afterwards.

A still better piece of fortune came to him when he was fourteen years of age. A schoolmaster named Matthew Coffin, who had taught the Haverhill District school when Greenleaf was one of the youngest scholars and had afterwards removed to another place, came for a short visit to Mr. Whittier's farm. In the evenings he read aloud to Mrs. Whittier and Aunt Mercy as they sat at their spinning when the day's work was done. Greenleaf never failed to make a third listener.

One night the visitor brought down into the family living room a little volume of Burns' poems and watched, as he read the verses, how the boy's face beamed with pleasure. The schoolmaster purposely left the book lying on the table, and before dawn next morning, Greenleaf was downstairs in the empty room poring over the pages and learning by heart one ballad after another. Here Mr. Coffin found him, and when the schoolmaster went away, he left the precious copy of Burns behind him that the boy might read and reread it at his leisure.

From that day a new interest came into the farm boy's life. He began to make verses himself. As he went about his work, everything he saw seemed to speak to him of some hidden beauty. The brook that flowed by the garden, the distant hills, the winding river Merrimack, the country sounds—all these pictures took shape in musical words and floated through his mind as he guided the plough or drove the cattle home from pasture in the evenings.

Long afterwards, when he had become a well-known poet, he wrote thus of this change that had taken place within him when a boy:

"I found that the things out of which poems came were not, as I had always imagined, somewhere far off in a world and life lying outside the edge of our own sky. They were right here about my feet and among the people I knew. The common things of our country life I found full of poetry."

Now, Greenleaf's father was a man who tried to do his duty by his children; but his mind was wholly given to the interests and work of each day. Poetry seemed foolishness to him, and for one of his boys to spend his time in writing poems would be, in his view, a sheer waste of life. Yet, if Greenleaf did his work thoroughly, he was free to spend his leisure as he chose. He worked hard in the fields like the other country boys about Haverhill, milked the cows, and carted home the pails of milk; and, so far as outward signs went, none of his companions could guess that he had any thoughts or dreams beyond those that satisfied their own daily lives. But when the work was done he began to write out in verse the thoughts that came to him, he knew not whence, and then arose the question where should he keep the store of treasures that slowly grew in size and that no one, as he thought, would ever care to read. The squirrels in the wood made storehouses for their nuts in the trunks of trees, but rain and wind would spoil a boy's papers if he put them in such a hiding place. At last, he thought of an unused attic under the farmhouse roof, and there this human squirrel found a hole behind some rubbish. This hole he made into his storehouse.

Little did he think as time went by that his secret hiding place was discovered. But this was the case, for his sister Mary began to notice how, in his holiday hours, Greenleaf was not to be seen as of old on Job's Hill or by the riverbank, and one day she saw him making his way up the dark, narrow stairs that only led to the unused attic in the roof. What could he want there, she wondered. Was it because he was unhappy that he seemed to need no companions and liked to wander away by himself? If so, she wanted to know his trouble, and it was not long before she, too, climbed the attic stairs, and there, in the hole in the wall, she found the store of verses. Probably the thought never entered

Mary Whittier's mind that she should ask leave before she read written papers that did not belong to her. These farmhouse dwellers were unused to literature, and the young people had few possessions of their own. However that might be, she sat down on the floor of the lonely room and read one poem after another till she had gone through the little heap, and then she began to think.

So that was what filled Greenleaf's thoughts, and her brother was really a poet! How hard it seemed that he never had a kind word from anyone about these verses and that no one ever read them. She said nothing to her brother, nor to anybody else, about the discovery she had made and puzzled over the matter till, at last, she made a plan by which she hoped to help him. We shall hear by and by what this plan was.

Meanwhile, a great event happened. Greenleaf went out to see the world. Some relatives in Boston asked him to visit them, and the Quaker boy went on his travels with warnings from his parents of the dangers that awaited him in the city and special command never to set foot inside a theater. His Aunt Mercy made him a broad-brimmed Quaker hat of pasteboard covered with dark velvet, and for the first time, his jacket was adorned with large buttons which surely, he thought, would cause all who passed him in the city streets to turn and gaze upon him. Needless to say, the country boy met with many wonderful experiences, but home influence and a tender conscience did not lose their power among these new impressions.

One evening, a stranger lady was at the supper table who was very kind and friendly to Greenleaf and talked to him as if she were an old acquaintance. To his surprise, he discovered she was an actress, and when she invited him to the theater on the following evening to see the play in which she was going to take a part, his surprise changed to horror. Obedient to what he thought would be the wish of his parents, next day he said goodbye to his relations, and, hurrying away from all the pleasures which his Boston visit still promised him, surprised the family circle at Haverhill by his unexpected return.

CHAPTER 3

THE FARM BOY'S HERO

The busy town of Newburyport lay on the Atlantic coast near the mouth of the river Merrimack, and once a week a postman rode thence into the district of Haverhill with letters and parcels for the country dwellers who were fortunate enough to have such messages sent to them from the outside world. Only a hedge separated the high road from the field at the back of Friend Whittier's farm, and if one of the farmer's boys happened to be working in the field when he heard the steady trot of the postman's pony coming down the hill, he used to throw aside his spade and straighten his back and rush to the hedge for a few words with the traveler.

The postman's arrival became a very important event in course of time; for Mr. Whittier began to take in a newspaper called the *Free Press*, which was published in Newburyport, and it came out to the farm once a week in the postman's bag. It is not too much to say that the paper seemed to bring fresh life into the farmhouse kitchen when it was read aloud at night. To Greenleaf it gave special delight, for there was a "Poet's Corner" in it, and he used to read eagerly every word of the poetry that was printed there.

One day a wonderful event took place. Greenleaf was helping his father to mend a stone wall that divided two of the fields when he heard the well-known trot of the pony on the hilly road. In another minute the rider had thrown the paper to him, and, according to his usual habit, Greenleaf looked first thing for the verses in the "Poet's Corner." What a strange sight did he see there!

He rubbed his eyes and looked again. For a moment his heart almost ceased to beat. There in print was one of his own poems which he had called "The Deity"—a poem which had been hidden in his treasure hole; and beneath the last verse was printed a short note from the editor of the paper saying that he would be glad to publish more poems written by the same pen!

How had this happened? Was he in dreamland? He stood still by the wall with his trowel lying at his feet and was recalled to the work-a-day world by his father's voice telling him to attend to his building. Certainly the broken wall must be mended, whatever news the *Free Press* might contain. There was no better worker on the farm than Greenleaf; indeed, sometimes he worked far beyond his strength, and in doing so he laid the seeds of future ill-health. He never let his love of poetry interfere with his duty. Throwing the paper aside, he began to place the heavy stones again, but still he pondered over the mystery and was still puzzling over it when he went to bed at night.

The solution of the puzzle lay in the loving heart of his elder sister Mary. She had formed a plan and carried it out, and here was the result. You must know that every week she had been in the habit of reading the verses in the newspaper that Greenleaf liked so much, and it seemed to her that the little store of his poems which she had found in their hiding place in the attic were no less worthy of insertion in the "Poet's Corner," and she resolved to copy one of them and send it to the office of the paper in Newburyport.

What a task she had set herself! Farmers' daughters in Haverhill, in those days, could spin and make butter and do all needful household work, but it was no easy matter to one of them to copy poetry. However, one day, when her brother was at work in the fields and all the rest of the household busy in various ways, she stole secretly up the unused flight of stairs, and with pale ink and bad pen—the best tools she could find—set to work to make a copy of "The Deity," the poem she liked the best of those that were hidden behind the rubbish heap. Slowly the pen traveled in the shaking hand, but at last the work was done. The verses lay before her in her cramped handwriting, which even she found difficult to read.

What was to be done next? After some consideration, Mary decided to take that important person, the weekly postman, into her confidence and to ask him to carry her packet to its destination at Newburyport. She had not the smallest doubt that she would see the poem in print in the *Free Press*, yet when the paper came with the editor's note to the unknown poet, her joy knew no bounds, and before long she felt obliged to tell her secret to Greenleaf.

Now, Friend Whittier and his family knew nothing about the editor of the *Free Press*. Perhaps if the honest Quaker had heard the story of the young man's life, he would have thought even more highly than he already did of his paper. For its editor, William Lloyd Garrison, was still little more than a boy, and but a few years had passed since he was a barefooted errand lad carrying baskets of chips for sale up and down the hilly streets of Newburyport for his master, Deacon Bartlett. The boy's father was a sea captain who had deserted his wife and family and gone no one knew whither. His mother was a nurse in a distant town, and while still quite small, Lloyd had begun to earn his own living, and his school days, in consequence, had been very few in number; but he had made the most of them, and when they were at an end, he could write better than any of his companions who had been far longer at school.

The young editor's boyhood was full of brave days that he was glad to look back upon. It was something to remember with joy now that his mother was dead, how when a wee lad he had vowed someday to make a home for her and had searched for work in all the shops and offices of the town, till a kindhearted printer of Newburyport had taken him as his apprentice while he was still too small to reach the high table on which the printing press stood. From that time all had gone well with him. He had come bravely out of the struggle. His master lent him money to set on foot a paper of his own, and thus the little barefooted boy who had sold chips in Newburyport became, in course of time, the editor of the town's newspaper.

If Lloyd Garrison was young, he was very outspoken and honest. He did not value his post chiefly as a means by which to earn a living. Through his paper he was able to bring good influences to bear on his native town, and this was what he cared for very greatly. Every week there came forth from his pen brave words to help on just causes; and never did he support a wrong side because it was popular nor keep silence when there was an evil to be redressed because it might injure the sale of his paper if he spoke out. This was why Friend Whittier liked the *Free Press* and cared to read it, though usually in his practical, hardworking life literature had few charms for him.

One morning when the editor came to his office, he found lying among his papers the little packet that the carrier had been good-natured enough to deliver for Mary Whittier. He picked it up and looked at it, noticed the faded ink and unformed handwriting, and, being very busy, was about to tear it up, when a second thought led him to look at it again and put it carefully on one side. For there came to him the memory of a day in his own struggling boyhood when he had written a paper with the greatest care and sent it unsigned to the printer, who was his master, for the chance that he might give it a place in the weekly paper that he published. He remembered how eagerly he had watched to see what would happen when his master opened his letters, and how he nearly cried out in his joy when the printer handed his own paper to him—then the youngest apprentice—to put it into print. Surely that piece of good fortune had made him the happiest boy, for the time, in the whole town. Remembering this incident, he would not now throw aside as a matter of no importance the childish-looking document that had come unsigned to him that busy morning.

By and by, Lloyd Garrison found time to spread out on his desk the verses from his unknown correspondent, and to decipher the cramped, faint letters. His interest grew as he read. "Who could this young poet be?" he asked himself. Plainly someone who had not had much practice writing. It must be some boy or girl who wanted encouragement and help—and deserved it, too, for these were verses of great promise. And so it came about that in the next week's number of the *Free Press* the boy's poem found a place, and within a month from that time, the unknown writer had replied to the editor's printed message by sending another poem for the "Poet's Corner."

Then Mr. Garrison began to wonder in good earnest what sort of a person this writer of poetry might be, and he made inquiries about the matter from the Haverhill carrier. In reply, he learned about Friend Whittier's farm and discovered that the mysterious poet was a boy working in his father's fields. He pictured to himself the farmer's lad plowing and digging and guessed that he might need a friend to help him to gain an education to develop his powers of mind. So he resolved that at the first opportunity he would take a holiday—a very rare event—and go to Haverhill to make a call at Friend Whittier's farm.

Early one summer morning, he set forth from Newbury-port, bent on carrying out this plan. A drive of many miles led him through pleasant country—at first by the sea coast, afterwards through meadows, whence he caught sight sometimes of the winding river. How bright the sunshine seemed and how fresh the country air to the dweller in the busy town! When distant blue hills at last came into view, he thought that, in truth, his young poet spent his life among beautiful surroundings. At the end of his journey, he drove down the steep road leading past the farm garden, and after fastening his horse at the gate, walked up the garden path and knocked at the house door.

Visitors were always kindly received at the farm, and Friend Whittier and his wife made no exception in the case of this pleasant-looking youth who did not look much older than their own son Greenleaf. It was surprising news to them to hear, as they soon did, that it was for the purpose of seeing Greenleaf that the stranger had taken the long drive from Newburyport.

"What has the boy been doing?" asked the farmer anxiously. He was not much relieved when he heard why the visitor wanted to speak to his son. However, one of the daughters was sent out into the fields to look for her brother, and then the talk went on.

"Poetry will never give him bread," was the farmer's next speech. When he had listened to Mr. Garrison's appeal that some chance of further education than he had yet had should be given to Greenleaf, he broke in with the hasty demand that no such foolish notions should be put into the boy's mind.

Meanwhile, Mary was running quickly into the fields to find her brother. "Surely some great future awaits him," she thought, "or else why should the editor of the *Free Press* come all the way from Newburyport to see him?" Greenleaf was at work, barefooted, in his shirt sleeves, digging potatoes. His sister told him her news breathlessly, and then found that he needed some persuasion before he would consent to go in to see the visitor. However, at last jacket and shoes were put on, and he entered the farmhouse kitchen. What was his surprise when he was greeted, not by a venerable man, but by a youth who spoke encouraging words to him about his verses such as he had never heard before, and greatly did he marvel when the stranger went on to urge his father to send him to school.

Not long afterwards Lloyd Garrison took his leave. Greenleaf watched him drive up the road and disappear from sight. Then he went back to the potato field and finished a good day's work. But fresh hopes had sprung up within him, and he felt a great longing to be what this new friend seemed to expect him to become. Still, he knew well that his father had no money to spare and that his work was needed on the farm; so he put resolutely away from his mind the bright vision of school days which had been suggested to him and allowed no daydreams to interfere with the duties that had to be done.

In a few months after his visit to the farm, Mr. Garrison left Newburyport and went to Boston. Then Greenleaf sent some verses to the *Haverhill Gazette*, a paper which was edited by Mr. Thayer of Haverhill and published in the little country town. And Mr. Thayer began, like Lloyd Garrison, to wonder what sort of a person the young poet, whom he knew nothing about, might be; and he, too, one day went to Friend Whittier's farm to see and talk with the farmer's son. Most exciting news did he bring with him. He told how, in the following summer, an Academy was to be opened in Haverhill, and offered to take Greenleaf to board for six months in his house that he might study at this new school, if the farmer would pay the school fees.

Friend Whittier had pondered much over the advice of Lloyd Garrison, and as time passed the objections he had raised to it vanished. Moreover, he saw with some anxiety that Greenleaf often worked beyond his strength on the farm. So he made no strong protest when Mr. Thayer proposed his scheme. Nothing could be settled then, however. That night the father and mother talked the matter over. There was a mortgage upon the farm and little sale for the timber in the wood or for the fruit and vegetables raised. Only want of means prevented them from sending their boy to study at the Academy. The next morning Greenleaf heard their decision and was told that if he could see how to earn his school fees there would be no other difficulty to overcome.

"Where there's a will, there's a way." Greenleaf began to make plans. The autumn passed, and the winter was at hand, when snow lay thick for a long time over the face of the earth, and no work could be done out of doors. Then Greenleaf's plans came to light.

CHAPTER 4

THE WILL AND THE WAY

It was the custom of many of the country people in the district of Haverhill to hire themselves out to work on the farms during the summer months and to follow some trade, such as that of a wheelwright or a shoemaker, in the winter. Among them was a good-natured farm laborer who worked for Friend Whittier and knew also how to make common shoes, which were sent to a distance to be sold. This man wondered much when his master's son came to him one day and asked him if he would teach him his trade that winter. He knew how well Greenleaf could work and agreed to do this; and so fast did the new apprentice learn his business that very soon he was paid eight cents for every pair of shoes he made.

All day long Greenleaf sat on his low bench working away at his shoemaking. As he stitched and hammered, beautiful thoughts came into his mind, and the verses which he wrote down in pencil he kept in a drawer beside his seat. By the end of the winter, he had earned enough money to pay his school fees. He was resolved that no extra expense on his account should fall on his father, and from that time he made it a rule never to buy anything for which he had not money to pay at once.

Meanwhile, the new Academy was built, and on April 18, 1827, the grand ceremony of opening the school was to take place. To celebrate the event, an Ode was read, which was said to have been composed by one of the future students; and, in truth, Greenleaf had written it as he sat on his cobbler's bench making shoes. We may safely guess that it was his friend Mr. Thayer who had made the Ode known to the managers of the Academy festival.

The following day Greenleaf took his place among the rest of the students. There were youths and maidens of various ages in the classes. Our poet was nineteen years old and tall for his age. But he was backward and ignorant, and, knowing this, felt not a particle of foolish pride when he found himself at first entered among the small boys. To work his hardest he was determined, for he did not know how few his school days might be. Soon he gained a higher place and then went on steadily rising. The scholars were, for the most part, farmers' sons like himself. It was not long before he held a position among them which no other youth in the Academy possessed. "He's the best of all the big fellows," was said of him by the younger boys, who were proud to be noticed by him in any way. The whole school began to delight in his verses, which were sometimes found written roughly on his slate and handed about from one to another.

By and by Greenleaf's admirers were not confined to the students of the Academy. A native poet was a very rare treasure in Haverhill, and the authorship of the poems in the *Free Press* and the *Haverhill Gazette*, which had been published anonymously, had become known. One of the chief inhabitants of Haverhill was Judge Minot. He and his family were attracted by the thoughtful face of young Whittier and began to invite him to join gatherings of a few of the neighbors who met for discussion at the judge's house on certain evenings each month. Greenleaf was naturally very silent, but he forgot his reserve and shyness on those occasions and entered with great zest into the talk. It is said that the farmer's son became the central figure at the judge's meetings, which never seemed complete if he were absent.

Greenleaf lived, as had been arranged, with Mr. Thayer's family. There was a good library in the house, and in the evenings when he came back from the Academy, he used to read diligently, so absorbed in his studies that though the children of the house romped round him he was not disturbed by their merry voices. Every Friday night he used to walk home to the farm to spend Sunday with his family and tell them all about what had happened to him during the past week.

Thus six months passed rapidly away. Meanwhile, Greenleaf had begun to ask himself somewhat anxiously the question: How was he to find money to pay for a second term at the Academy? It happened that a schoolmaster was wanted in the neighboring village of West Amesbury during the following winter months, and Greenleaf offered himself for the post. His handwriting was good; the managers asked few questions and gave him the appointment. So he became sole master for a room full of rough country lads who at first showed little respect for their young teacher. They did all they could to provoke him. Some of them were bright and clever enough to puzzle him with the questions they asked him, and he spent many an hour late at night, when he should have been asleep, over problems in mathematics which he would have to explain on the following day. It was a bitterly cold winter, and he needed warm clothes which he had no money to buy; but what did hardships matter to him? He was earning his education, and his old father would not have a cent to pay for his Academy fees next term.

When that term came, and he was back in his place among the students, none of them worked harder than he did. To earn a little money, he used to post up the ledgers of a storekeeper in Haverhill every week, and he still found time in the evenings for a great amount of reading in Mr. Thayer's library, in addition to his needful classwork. At the end of the term, he graduated; life at the Academy was over, and he went home to work in the fields and milk the cows, as he had done before his student life began. About sixty years afterwards, Greenleaf Whittier was present at a gathering of the few survivors among the students who had been at Haverhill Academy in the last term, and he read the following poem, which he had written for the occasion:

THE REUNION

The gulf of seven-and-fifty years
We stretch our welcoming hands across;
The distance but a pebble's toss
Between us and our youth appears.

For in life's school we linger on,
The remnant of a once full list;
Conning our lessons, undismissed,
With faces to the setting sun.

And some have gone the unknown way,
And some await the call to rest;
Who knoweth whether it is best
For those who went or those who stay?

And yet despite of loss and ill,
If faith and love and hope remain,
Our length of days is not in vain,
And life is well worth living still.

Still to a gracious Providence,
The thanks of grateful hearts are due;
For blessings when our lives were new,
For all the good vouchsafed us since.

'Tis something that we wander back,
Gray pilgrims, to our ancient ways;
And tender memories of old days
Walk with us by the Merrimack:

That even in life's afternoon
A sense of youth comes back again,

As through this cool September rain
The still green woodlands dream of June.

* * * *

Dear comrades, scattered wide and far
Send from their homes their kindly word;
And dearer ones unseen, unheard,
Smile on us from some heavenly star.

For life and death with God are one,
Unchanged by seeming change His care
And love are round us here and there,
He breaks no thread His hand has spun.

Soul touches soul, the muster roll
Of life eternal has no gaps;
And after half a century's lapse
Our school-day ranks are closed and whole.

Hail and farewell! We go our way
Where shadows end we trust in light;
The star that ushers in the night
Is herald also of the day!

As he went about his work on the farm, Greenleaf often pondered over his future. Indeed, it was a question which puzzled the whole family, for they knew nothing about the openings in life which a youth might find in the busy world that lay beyond their sheltering hills. The end of the year 1828 was at hand.

Fortunately, William Lloyd Garrison had not forgotten the farm boy at Haverhill. He had often inquired about him and had heard how he earned his school fees—first by shoemaking and afterwards as a schoolmaster—and of his success as a student at

Haverhill Academy. When the news reached him that Greenleaf had graduated and gone back to work on the farm, he used his influence to gain for him a post in a Boston printing office, knowing that he would have chances in the city of carrying on his education. So it came to pass that, in December 1828, Mr. Garrison sent word to Greenleaf that if he would apply for the situation, Messrs. Collier and Son, of Boston, would probably employ him to write articles for their paper, *The American Manufacturer*, for which he would receive a small salary. He would have ample time to read in a public library in Boston and pursue his own studies.

This was good fortune, indeed; and Friend Whittier and his wife thought so. Still more glad were they to hear the news that there was room for their son to board in the house in Boston in which Lloyd Garrison made his home.

At the beginning of the New Year, Greenleaf said goodbye again to his family and home and began his new life in the printing office. Out of the meager salary he received, he managed not only to support himself but also to put aside half the sum toward freeing his father's farm from debt.

One can picture the life this youth of twenty years now led. Before writing each newspaper article, he had to study its subject; but every hour spent in the quiet library was a delight to him, and his reading there did even more for the training of his mind than his work at the Academy had done. Through his connection with the newspaper for which he wrote, he became acquainted with some of the leaders in Boston politics—men of experience and position—who gladly talked sometimes with the promising young, rising writer and prophesied a useful future before him. But best of all the influences of that time was the influence of Lloyd Garrison upon him. Greenleaf had looked upon this youth, so little older than himself, as a pioneer and leader ever since that summer day when he had visited the farm and opened, as it were, a new doorway in life before the country boy.

Garrison was at this time engaged in editing *The National Philanthropist*, a Boston paper. It was the first Temperance paper ever published in the United States; and young Whittier reverenced his hero more and more as he read in it the brave words with which he fearlessly inveighed against the drinking customs of the time and tried to waken the sleeping consciences of the citizens concerning any evil that needed to be reformed, regardless of the effect on his own reputation.

To walk at night on Boston Common and talk with Garrison about the great themes that filled his thoughts was a joy to Greenleaf. The snow lay on the ground, and the wind whistled drearily round them; but their enthusiasm kept them warm, and they never heeded the weather. It was the influence of this brave friend that most of all made Whittier long to help forward the great causes that needed support. He did not doubt that he must go on writing poems and try to put into words that beauty that he saw lying around him—he was a poet by nature—but, as they tramped over the lonely common together, he used to say to Garrison that he, too, must fight against the evil in the world, and that he was resolved to try before he died to deserve the name most worth having—the name of "friend of man."

Now, Lloyd Garrison, in his turn, had heroes whose example led him up and on and helped him to be strong and fearless. Of one of these heroes he had heard from his boyhood, but had never seen him. His name was Benjamin Lundy. He had been cast, a friendless orphan boy of Quaker parentage, on the world to make a living as he could. Hardworking and honest, he began to prosper after a long struggle with difficulties, and became a saddler in a town on the bank of the river Ohio, in the state of Virginia. The window near which he sat working at his trade looked on the road which led to the river, and now and then he saw terrible sights on this road, the remembrance of which haunted him day and night. Gangs of miserable slaves, chained together, on their way to plantations farther South, were driven past his door. He could see their hopeless faces and hear the driver's lash, and at last he could no longer rest contentedly in his home, where he had a dearly-loved wife and children. Pity drove him out into the world to try what he could do in some small way to right the cruel wrongs to the slaves. When he had made enough money to enable his family to support themselves, he sold his business and set on foot a newspaper which should spread abroad the story of the horrors of the Slave Trade. He had to walk twenty miles to find a printer every week, and when his paper was printed, he used to tramp about the country with a heavy pack of papers on his back, selling them as he went on his way. Month after month and year after year, his life went on thus. His wife died; his children were scattered. He grew old and feeble, and still he toiled on to help the friendless slaves.

Most unexpectedly, to the very house in which Lloyd Garrison and Greenleaf Whittier were living during the winter of 1828, this same Benjamin Lundy came and asked for a lodging for a few nights. And now, for the first time, Garrison saw his hero—an insignificant-looking, bent old man, worn and deaf, yet full of enthusiasm for his work. He had come to Boston to call a meeting of all the clergymen in the town and beg them to help him to form an Anti-Slavery Society there. Now Boston, like other cities in the northern states, was opposed to the institution of slavery; but Boston men were, many of them, afraid to offend the South if they made any public stand against slaveholding. Only eight clergymen attended the meeting. But Benjamin Lundy spoke such thrilling words there that Garrison's "soul was set on fire," and that night he buckled on his armor and resolved to fight against slavery and the slave trade till he died or the land was freed from the curse of such a wrong.

Benjamin Lundy went on his lonely way. Very soon an opening came for Garrison to begin his war against slavery by editing an influential paper in Vermont, in which he could speak his mind out on the subject. Whittier and he parted, and for a long time, they did not meet again, but this six months' companionship had been a grand training for Greenleaf. Could he fail hereafter to live an earnest life, or forget the examples of brave faithfulness set him by Garrison and Benjamin Lundy? He ventured to send a letter after his hero, praying him to be of good courage and to be sure that there were great things waiting for him to do. This letter gladdened Garrison.

Not long after Lloyd Garrison's departure from Boston, Greenleaf began to receive letters which made him anxious about his father's health and led him to feel sure that it was time that he should go back to the farm and his old place at home.

The news did not improve; and when he wrote proposing to return, the answer showed him how welcome he would be. Therefore, he left Boston with as little delay as possible; and when he saw his father and found how the old man's strength was beginning to fail, he resolved never to leave him again and to take upon himself all the burdens that had begun to press heavily upon him. By this time Uncle Moses was dead, and Greenleaf's younger brother Matthew had left home and was a clerk in a distant town, so the oversight of the farm had fallen on the old farmer. To his mother, aunt, and sisters, it was a great joy to have Greenleaf at home again, and a heavy load of anxiety was taken off their minds when they saw how Friend Whittier trusted in his son and began to take the rest he so much needed.

As for Greenleaf, his Boston life began quickly to seem like a dream. He took up again the old work of plowing and digging and cheered his father with fresh plans for making money and paying off the mortgage on the farm. It was a difficult matter to sell the farm produce. Once or twice a week he began to drive a cart laden with vegetables and fruit to the bank of the Merrimack, where ships came up with the tide. There the captains were ready to exchange salt fish for his goods, or to carry them down as cargo to the mouth of the river where the townspeople gladly bought them. When the day's work outside the house was done, Greenleaf still went on earning. He obtained the post of editor of a Haverhill paper, and the salary thus earned was added to the savings, which it was hoped would in time free the land from debt.

In the east window of the farmhouse kitchen there stood an ancient desk that had belonged to the family since the days of Greenleaf's great-grandfather, the son of the pioneer, Thomas Whittier. Here Greenleaf wrote his articles for the paper and his early poems, few of which have been preserved. He wrote about simple scenes in home life and everyday interests which were familiar to the poorest country people in the land; but he gave a fresh aspect to them all so that the readers of his verses saw a new loveliness and a sacredness in the old familiar scenes and customs. One thing more must be told about his life at this time. His sister Elizabeth, who was eight years younger than himself and had been his special pet in childhood, was now his closest, dearest companion, who could enter into all his thoughts and take delight in his poems. Thus autumn and winter passed, and another spring came and went; and in June 1830, Friend Whittier was gathered to his fathers and Greenleaf became the head of the family. Meanwhile, he was really injuring his health with the hard work he did, but so unselfish and cheerful was he that no one suspected it.

CHAPTER 5

A SUMMONS TO BATTLE

Greenleaf's labors at the old desk in the evenings increased. He was invited to send essays and poems to the *New England Review*, a paper with a large circulation in Connecticut. He began to receive long letters from the editor, Mr. George D. Prentice, asking his advice about matters connected with the paper, Mr. Prentice believing, as it appeared afterwards, that his correspondent was a man of mature years. One day, Greenleaf was hoeing a potato field when the carrier brought him a letter containing most surprising news. Mr. Prentice wrote to say that he was obliged to leave Connecticut for a time, and that he had advised the leading men of the state, who owned the *New England Review*, to send for Greenleaf Whittier to take his place as its editor. Now, this was the chief paper of Connecticut, and Greenleaf was only a youth of twenty-three years of age. "I should not have been more astonished," he said in later years, "if I had heard I had been appointed Prime Minister to the Khan of Tartary." A good salary was offered to him. It would be a grand way to earn money, far better than by farming, but it was not long since his father died, and he was wanted at home. Besides, though he had had a little experience in political life in Boston, the post now offered to him was a most important one, and he felt his youth and inexperience keenly.

What was he to do? What answer should he send? After two or three sleepless nights, he talked the matter over with his mother, and she advised him to accept the post. Once more Greenleaf left the old home and went out into the world.

The stagecoach, jolting over rough roads, carried him to Hartford, the chief town in the state of Connecticut. There were only two railroads at that time in the whole of the United States, and none in New England where Haverhill and Hartford both lay. As intercourse with the outside world was somewhat difficult, one might expect to find Hartford a dull, sleepy place. On the contrary, its inhabitants were wide awake, and the members of the Legislature and the chief citizens were preparing for the approaching nomination of candidates to the presidency of the United States and just about to enter into a fierce political campaign.

These political leaders did not lose time in visiting the newly appointed editor of the *New England Review*. To their great surprise they found, seated in the editor's chair, a youth in homespun clothes of Quaker cut, who was far more ready to listen than to speak. Could this be the noted John Greenleaf Whittier into whose care they had given their chief paper? Doubtless there was much shaking of heads and sinking of hearts among them at first, but their despondency lasted only for a short time. They discovered that behind the boyish, country-looking exterior there lay a strong character, that their new editor had courage to stand by his opinions and to be firm and true to principle, and possessed plenty of energy and common sense.

Strange experiences awaited young Whittier. There was strong party feeling in the town, and the opponents of the *New England Review* scoffed at his youth and inexperience; and, thinking thus to prove his unfitness for his post, set on foot a story in the town that he had earned his living at a cobbler's bench. Greenleaf was not in the least ashamed of this fact, but he dreaded ridicule and public notice and sometimes heartily wished he could hide himself out of sight of men.

One day, as he opened one of the "exchange papers" regularly sent to the office, he caught sight of his own name heading a long article. He read it and to his dismay found it was an abusive and scornful criticism of himself and his work as editor. This was very hard to bear, and for some days he lived in dread of finding the article copied into other papers. He did not dare speak of it to anyone but went about with a heavy load on his heart, which he bore in silence. At length he summoned courage to write to his reviler and ask for fair play. But all the answer he received was an expression of contempt because he was so "thin skinned," and a warning that he would receive far worse treatment in course of time.

Greenleaf was no coward, but he very naturally feared that such untruthful attacks might injure his influence. They came to an end before long, however, and did him no real harm; in fact, they helped to strengthen his character. He grew more self-reliant and threw himself eagerly into the political struggle that was agitating the country, doing good work by his leaders and articles in the *Review*. Friendly notices of him began to appear in other papers, and he received invitations to call upon editors in New York and Boston. He was always outspoken in whatever he wrote, never feared to oppose what he did not agree with, yet he never failed in courtesy to his opponents and won for himself a high position in the town of Hartford. His first volume of poems came out about this time. It was published in the office of the *Review*.

Though Greenleaf still wrote verses, his daydreams were no longer to rank among the poets of the land. His life in Hartford had changed his aims. He became ambitious for political power, longed for a career as a statesman and to climb to a place among the leaders in the land. The owners of the paper were delighted with the "push" and courage of their ambitious young editor; and when he found that affairs connected with his late father's estate obliged him to return for a time to Haverhill, they valued him too much to part with him, and it was arranged that he should write letters and articles for the *New England Review* during his stay at home. So we may picture him again by day overlooking and working on the farm, and in the evenings writing busily at the old desk in the kitchen, his mind centered on the course of politics in Hartford which, through the columns of the paper, he was helping powerfully to form and guide.

The dawn of the year 1832 brought both good and evil fortune to Greenleaf. By that time he had saved enough money to pay off the mortgage on the farm, and this was a great satisfaction to him, for thereby the chief wish of his dear old father was fulfilled. But at the same time came a breakdown in his health. He became too ill to carry on his work at Hartford and had to resign his post there. The fact was, he was feeling the result of years of overwork on the farm, and many months had to pass before he regained a fair amount of health.

Nearly three years had gone by since Greenleaf Whittier and Lloyd Garrison had parted in Boston. A rough path had, meanwhile, opened out before Garrison's willing feet. He was using every chance that came his way to battle against slavery, and such efforts could not fail to lead him into danger. Something of what had happened to him may now be told. Startling news had reached him one day—news that filled him with the fiercest indignation. A proposal was made by certain senators sent up to Congress by the Southern States that the United States should go to war with Mexico for the purpose of wresting from Mexico the great free lands of Texas on which slave states should be formed and added to the slave states already in the Union.

Why did not the people of the free North at once rise up to protest against this scheme? This was what Garrison demanded; and indignant with the apathy and silence around him, he declared there was no courage and no faithfulness left in the land and spoke and wrote such vehement words against the sinfulness of the slave traffic that cowardly men in the Northern States feared the anger of the South. So a cry was raised that "Madcap Garrison" must be silenced. And silenced he was for a time; for an action for libel was brought against him by a Newburyport merchant whom he had publicly and justly accused of carrying a cargo of slaves in his ship, and since Garrison could not pay the fine imposed upon him, he was imprisoned in the jail at Baltimore, where he was then living.

This news reached Whittier at the Haverhill farm, and straightway he made urgent appeals on Garrison's behalf to a wealthy statesman whom he knew. While the statesman still hesitated, a New York merchant paid the fine, and "Madcap Garrison" was a free man again. One of the poems written about this time by Whittier at his ancestor's desk was addressed to his hero.

By and by more tidings of Garrison reached Haverhill. He was traveling through the States on foot delivering lectures against slavery, notwithstanding repeated warnings that he must be silent if he valued his life. The brave youth's only reply was that he was bound to do the work to which he was called and would leave the results to God. His next step was to establish himself in a cheerless garret in Boston as his home and printing office. There, with no subscribers and no capital, he began to publish a little anti-slavery paper called *The Liberator*, and still his cry always was, "I am in earnest; I will not equivocate, I will not excuse, I will not retreat a single inch, and I will be heard." Thus he lighted the spark which grew into a mighty flame, and week by week he fanned the flame and never heeded the threats and abuse that were poured forth against him. Was it any wonder that Greenleaf Whittier reverenced him?

It is an old story now—that terrible story about the anti-slavery struggle in the United States; and many pages in history have been turned since those days when the storm which was to break over the land was just beginning to rise in the cities of the North. But it is a story which should never be forgotten, for heroes were concerned in it who never faltered in defending the right, though all odds were against them, and they should serve as leaders and encouragers for those who have to battle against wrong of any kind in all times to come.

Slave labor and the slave trade date back to the landing of the Pilgrim Fathers in America. Slavery became an institution of the country. The great cotton plantations of the South depended upon slave labor. Men grew rich by importing and rearing slaves, and it was not till the slave trade suddenly began to increase and the system of slavery threatened to spread beyond the old accustomed boundary line into the free land of the North, that the need arose for heroes to declare that this national institution was a sin.

But the Northern States bought the cotton raised on the slave plantations of the South, and to cease to buy it meant ruin to the Northern mill owners. Moreover, it was said that to free the slaves would imperil their masters' lives; also, that free men would not cultivate the cotton on the dismal swamps. Above all, it was urged that if the Northerners cried out against the sin of slavery, they would bitterly offend the people of the Southern States and endanger the Union of the North and South. So, for the sake of expediency and safety, "Madcap Garrison," and men like him, were to be silenced.

Lloyd Garrison's little messenger, *The Liberator*, began to make its way far and wide through the Northern States and down into the South. In answer came offers of large rewards to anyone who would kidnap Garrison and bring him into the Southern States for trial. The little paper was bought and read in the streets of Boston; and, as if in contemptuous reply, the building of new factories for the manufacture of slave-grown cotton went on rapidly in the city. There was no time to be lost. More helpers in the cause of freedom were needed; and Garrison, calling to mind the talks he had had with Greenleaf Whittier during their walks on Boston Common, wrote to urge him to examine for himself into the question of slavery and see if he did not feel bound to enroll himself in the little army that was waging war against it.

A word from Garrison was enough. Very soon on Greenleaf's

desk lay a pile of books and papers. One by one, he read them carefully through and came to the conclusion that he must answer "Yes" to Garrison's appeal. But see what a great trial lay before him! It was true that, owing to ill-health, he was living for a time in retirement on the farm, but he had fixed his hopes on going back into political life. He was filled with great ambitions. He had resolved to make his mark in the world both by his writings and his active service to the State. He had grown to love intensely the stir and excitement of political life. He was longing for the joy of entering again into the service of his country in this way, and he thought he saw before him the promise of a great career.

To do as Garrison implored him to do would put an end to all these dreams. To enroll himself among the despised and hated anti-slavery workers would ruin his chances of popularity as a poet and a newspaper editor. His cherished ambitions would have to be laid aside. No wonder that a great struggle took place within him between duty and inclination. Long years afterwards, when he was an old man, he laid his hand upon the head of a boy who had not yet reached the parting of the ways in his life, and said to him, "My lad, if thou wouldst win success, join thyself to some unpopular but noble cause."

Well, Greenleaf thought over the matter, and he knew that the right must win and that duty must be done at all costs. He took the first step and wrote a powerful pamphlet entitled "Justice and Expediency," in which he pointed out the injustice of slavery and the necessity for the immediate emancipation of the slaves. This pamphlet he published at his own expense, using for the purpose a large part of the savings of years.

The first step thus taken, the way opened out before him. But from that time, for many years, he had a hard struggle to keep out of debt and support the little family. He undertook some bookkeeping to earn money, for he no longer hoped that his writings would bring him an income. From this time there was a change in the poems he wrote. They were no longer the graceful popular verses that had been copied week by week in newspapers and admired by hosts of readers. They rang now like the fiery words of a prophet. "He became the voice for which a few had been wearily waiting, yet which exasperated and terrified the whole country." He called the poems which he began to write from this time "Voices of Freedom," and they were like trumpet blasts following each other in quick succession. Garrison had, indeed, called a brave warrior into the field.

CHAPTER 6

BUCKLING ON ARMOR

One autumn day in the year 1833, six months after Greenleaf had published his anti-slavery pamphlet, a messenger from Boston appeared at the farmhouse as twilight and mist were settling down upon the hills and meadows at Haverhill. He was invited to enter and lost no time in telling his business. Mr. Garrison had sent him with an urgent message to Greenleaf Whittier asking him to come to Philadelphia within a few days to help himself and a little company of resolute men to form a National Anti-Slavery Society and hold the first meeting in that town.

Now, Philadelphia lay on the borderland of slavery, so the proposed undertaking was full of danger, but that was of no consequence. There was a real difficulty, however, in Greenleaf's way. In the present state of his affairs, he could not afford the expense of the journey, and this was the answer he was obliged to send. Speedily that obstacle was overcome, for there were one or two wealthy men interested in the scheme who were ready to furnish money to help the workers. Word was sent to him that all costs would be gladly paid; so, as soon as he could make arrangements for the care of the farm during his absence, he set forth by stagecoach to meet Lloyd Garrison and travel with him to Philadelphia.

Other men, bound on the same errand, joined them on the way, and when their journey was ended, a number of them met together to make plans for the public meeting the next day. Far into the night Garrison and Whittier sought through the town for some well-known citizen who would be willing to act as president. All in vain. No one would risk his reputation in such a service. The chair had to be taken by one of their own party—a stranger to the city.

Early the following morning, a mob of roughs gathered outside the doors of the room where the meeting was to be held, ready to greet all who entered with abuse and mockery. Picture the scene inside the room! Only an assembly of some sixty men, mostly young, some of them farmers in homespun clothes, others in Quaker dress, with resolute air and earnest faces, and a few women, who were ready to give their lives and all they owned to help to free the slaves; Garrison the leader of them all, and among them the poet, John Greenleaf Whittier, their newly elected secretary.

A "Declaration of Principles" was laid upon a table, which was to be signed by all present at the close of the meeting. Solemnly and silently, one by one, they set their names to the paper. It was no light matter to do so; for then and there they pledged themselves, among other promises, to form anti-slavery societies in every city in the land, to send forth lecturers to rouse public attention, and to spare no pains to put an end to the national sin of slave-holding. "I set a higher value on my name as appended to the Anti-Slavery Declaration of 1833 than to the title page of any book," said Whittier, in old age, as he looked back over the events of a long life. The signing of that pledge, which seemed at the time to ensure the ruin of his most cherished projects, proved to be, in the end, the act which he recalled with greater satisfaction than any other in his life.

Thus pledged to give time and strength to the anti-slavery cause, Greenleaf went back to the farm, resolved to strain every nerve to keep his promise. He set to work to form an anti-slavery society among the people who had known him all his life, acting himself as secretary. There was strong pro-slavery feeling in the district, and the society found little favor; but since everyone respected young Whittier, he met with less open opposition than might have been expected, and, notwithstanding his support of a most unpopular cause, he was twice sent from Haverhill as representative to the State Legislature.

When Greenleaf was a boy, his favorite hero was Greatheart in the *Pilgrim's Progress*. In his youth, as we know, he looked upon Lloyd Garrison as his leader. In his view, the highest kind of courage was moral courage—not physical bravery merely, but the courage that makes a man stand true to principle and duty whatever the cost, ready to risk all that is dear in life for the sake of what is right. This was the sort of courage he longed to make his own. It was a brave deed when the young farmer again and again, after his day's work was done, sat down at his desk to pen a "Song of Freedom," which, bearing his name, was to travel far and wide over the land. Of one of these songs it was said that he had "seized the great trumpet of Liberty and blown a blast which should ring from Maine to the Rocky Mountains." Each of these blasts on Whittier's trumpet gave new courage to anti-slavery workers and hastened on the day of victory.

The years 1834 and 1835 were known in America as "the great mob years." Popular feeling by that time was so strong against the Abolitionists that anyone who was suspected of sympathy with the slaves lived in constant danger of losing his property and even his life. It had become a crime to teach a black person to read or to hide a runaway slave from the master, who was on his track to carry him back again to bondage from the free North to which he had escaped. The report that an anti-slavery meeting was about to be held in any town was the signal for a gathering round the place of an assembly of roughs who were always ready for any chance to break out into violence, knowing well that for such an outburst the authorities would be slow to call them to order. At such times the streets were filled rapidly by the mob, whose weapons were brickbats and stones, and who did not hesitate, if the chance came, to tar and feather or hang on the spot, any man against whom their rage was turned. No one who had been a spectator of one of such riots could ever forget the terrible sight. More than one such experience fell to the lot of Greenleaf Whittier and his young sister Elizabeth, and the story of these events must now be told.

It must be borne in mind that the chief town in each state of the Union possessed a House of Legislature, to which representatives were sent up from various districts in the State to discuss and manage public business. Thus, in Boston, the chief city in Massachusetts, stood the State House on Beacon Hill; and when the people of Haverhill chose Greenleaf Whittier to represent them in the councils of the State, it was his duty to spend some time in Boston that he might confer with representatives from other parts of Massachusetts in the State House. It happened that at one time he took with him his dear companion and sister, "Lizzie," and she stayed with him at the house of an old friend, the Rev. S.J. May, who, like Greenleaf, was hard at work in the anti-slavery cause.

Lizzie, who always entered so heartily into her brother's thoughts, had by this time thrown herself heart and soul into his anti-slavery interests. When she heard that certain ladies in Boston were to hold the annual meeting of their small anti-slavery society in the city, she resolved to go there while Greenleaf was about his business in the State House. The meeting was to take place in a little room separated by a wooden partition from Mr. Garrison's printing office, and notices had been placarded on the walls of Boston that the editor of *The Liberator* would give an address.

It was three o'clock on an October afternoon. The people of the town were going about their business in the sunny streets when these brave Boston ladies took their seats. Among them were several black women. Elizabeth Whittier was there, eager for her first experience of such a meeting, when, through the open window, came the sound of fierce, strong voices and of heavy footsteps hurrying in the street below. In another minute up the narrow staircase pushed angry, scowling men who fought their way into the room to glare upon the ladies quietly seated within it. The sight of Mr. Garrison in their midst was the signal for a storm of howls and hisses. Stones were thrown through the window by the crowd beneath, and yells broke out as Mr. Garrison advanced to address the rioters. For the sake of his own safety, and the safety of all concerned, the president begged him to retire out of sight into his own office, and for a moment there was a hush as, in calm, clear words, she began her opening prayer by thanking God that though there were so many to molest them none could make them afraid. But the silence was short; the shrieks and blasphemy were renewed, and a fresh storm of stones dashed through the broken window panes. One or two of the ladies were struck.

Suddenly, a cry was raised that the mayor was at hand. Tramp, tramp came the sound of steadily marching feet, and a company of police, headed by the mayor, forced their way through the mob, clearing the staircase and making a safe passage for the ladies to leave the meeting.

"Go home, ladies!" cried the Mayor. "Go home, if you would not see bloodshed. I can protect you now; in a little while, it will be impossible." They passed down into the street and through the howling, hooting crowd, two abreast—the calm, brave white women of gentle birth, walking beside their black sisters to secure their safety; and the mob closing up again, swaying, surging, and yelling, waited for Garrison to appear.

Meanwhile, the news of the riot was quickly carried through the city and reached the State House. Greenleaf, to whom the thought of his sister's danger lent wings, sped down the hilly streets, and when he found her in safety, he hurried on to *The Liberator* office, anxious for Garrison's life. Mayor and constables notwithstanding, the rioters had seized him and were dragging him through the streets by a rope round his body with intent to hang him. He was rescued with great difficulty and lodged for the night in the city jail, where Mr. May and Greenleaf Whittier gained entrance to him. The story of this Boston riot is preserved in the annals of the city. Not a few other towns in the United States have similar histories to recount.

But it was not only in cities that the anti-slavery workers met with ill-treatment. This was their fate often in country districts like the valley of the Merrimack, where farm houses nestled among the hills, and quiet little country towns such as Haverhill were scarce. After Greenleaf had formed his small society among the people of Haverhill, it became the custom at times for lecturers to come from Boston and elsewhere to give addresses there. These lecturers were always entertained at the Whittiers' farmhouse. On one occasion, when all the family, except Elizabeth, were from home, the Rev. S.J. May, who was one of the best known anti-slavery lecturers, came from Boston, according to agreement, to lecture one Sunday evening in the Baptist Church in Haverhill.

Elizabeth, not yet grown to womanhood, was delighted to act as hostess to her brother's old friend, and went with him to the meeting. The church was filled with people; and the audience, spellbound by the lecturer's eloquence, did not hear any disturbance in the road outside till they were suddenly warned by heavy stones thrown through the windows that the building was besieged by enemies. The terrified congregation rose and hurried away, unhurt by the mob of men and boys who waited, with a loaded cannon, for the lecturer's appearance. He urged Elizabeth in vain to leave him and seek safety with the rest. She would not listen to his requests. A girl friend as brave as herself insisted on staying with him; and each of them, taking one of Rev. May's hands, passed with him through the church door into the full view of the riotous crowd. A roar of vexation went up from numbers of hoarse throats. Elizabeth Whittier and her friend, Judge Minot's daughter, were well-known, and the men fell back, ashamed and afraid to carry out their purpose. Thus Mr. May's life was saved.

Strangely enough, that same evening Greenleaf also was in danger from a similar cause. In the company of George Thompson, a famous orator who had come from England to help forward the struggling anti-slavery cause in the United States, he had gone to Concord, near Boston, to hold a meeting in the courthouse. This meeting was never held. Early in the evening, in the streets of Concord, gathered a crowd of men shouting and throwing stones and mud. It was useless to open the courthouse doors. Whittier, his friend, and their host were discovered and pelted. They were separated, and Whittier, wounded in the face, heard a cry raised in the dark, "They've killed the Englishman, and now they are going for the Quaker!" Friendly hands drew him into a house for shelter; but guns were firing in the streets, and he was anxious for the safety of his friends. Changing his Quaker hat for a borrowed one, he went out among the rioters. Musket barrels shone in the moonlight. If he had been discovered, they would have been turned upon him, but the crowd was frenzied with drink.

During the night, by dint of great efforts on the part of their friends in Concord, Greenleaf and his English companion were rescued from their peril and driven at a gallop into the open country. After some hours of traveling, they reached the Haverhill farm in safety. A story is told about this homeward drive which shows what a keen sense of humor Greenleaf Whittier possessed. The travelers stopped to rest their horse and breakfast at a roadside inn. The landlord told them about the disturbance at Haverhill and how it had ended. In the course of their talk, one of the unknown travelers asked him:

"What kind of fellow is this Whittier?"

"Oh! He's an ignorant sort of chap—a Quaker farmer."

"And who is this Thompson they're talking about?"

"Him! He's a man sent over by the British government to make trouble between the North and South."

Just as they were driving away, Mr. Whittier turned to the landlord and said: "You have been talking about Thompson and Whittier. This is Mr. Thompson, and I am Whittier. Good morning." Telling the story afterwards, he added: "We jumped into the carriage and stood not on the order of our going. For all I know, he (the landlord) is standing there still with his mouth open."

CHAPTER 7

IN THE MIDST OF THE STRIFE

When life is full of purpose and interest the flight of time is almost unheeded. This was the case at the farmhouse, where not only Greenleaf Whittier, but all the household, were intent on the great struggle that was in the course of time to rend the country. Greenleaf, hard at work as one of the secretaries of the National Anti-Slavery Association, lecturing, writing for the papers, getting up petitions to Congress, attending conventions in various towns, and busy in a vast amount of public work of many kinds, was leaving youth behind him and entering upon middle age. His mother and Aunt Mercy were silver-haired, and they began to show signs of needing, more than they had hitherto done, the tender care and thought he always bestowed upon them. Matthew and Mary Whittier had both been sometime married and had homes and interests of their own. Lizzie, Greenleaf's youngest sister, brightened the old house and was full of merriment. Dearly did the quiet, overly weighted man enjoy his young sister's fun. He used to listen to her talk and sit rubbing his hands and laughing with the greatest enjoyment at her ready wit. Grave thinkers and workers who came to consult him and talk over the work in which they were all engaged found her a sunbeam in his quiet home. But there was another side to Lizzie's character. She was a lover of all that was beautiful; and Greenleaf turned to her constantly, and never in vain, for sympathy in the aspirations and ideals of his poetic nature.

Our story must now tell of great changes that took place in the life of the Whittier family. The day came when it was found needful that the dear old home, which had been built two hundred years before by their English ancestors, should pass into the possession of strangers. Greenleaf was obliged to be so often absent that there were intervals when he could not overlook the work on the farm, and he would not let the burden rest on his mother and aunt. Moreover, the long drive on "First-days" to the meeting house at Amesbury was too great an exertion for them now.

So the farmhouse was sold, and with it the acres of meadowland around it, and the family removed to a cottage at Amesbury. This was the home of Greenleaf Whittier for many years to come.

Of all the family, Lizzie felt the most grief at the removal. It was especially painful to her to leave the little garden by the brook, which had belonged to her since she was a child, and the fields where she used to find the earliest wildflowers.

"I wonder if I shall ever love Amesbury and its people," she said. "I shall when I forget the dear ones and things at Haverhill, perhaps. I know scarce any one of the abolition people there, but expect to like them all—or at least their abolition." From which it may be seen how deep a hold the anti-slavery crusade had on her mind. And here it may be said that very soon after her settlement at Amesbury, Elizabeth Whittier became President of the first Women's Anti-Slavery Society in the little town.

The new cottage home was only one story high. At one end of the building lay the "garden-room." This was considered to be Greenleaf's study, but it was used also for the family sitting room, for he always liked to write and read with his friends about him. The windows of the room overlooked the garden where pear trees and grapevines flourished.

Amesbury was a quiet place, surrounded by meadows and orchards. A few hundred yards from the cottage stood the Friends' Meeting House, where the Whittier children had often in old days gone to worship with their parents from the farm at

Haverhill. It was in this village, too, that Greenleaf had once been a "Winter Schoolmaster" when he wanted to earn money for his Academy fees. Below the hill on which Amesbury lay flowed the river Merrimack, and across the river were hills and woods which afforded a fine view from the cottage.

During those years of storm and stress of which our story now tells, it did not fall to the lot of Greenleaf Whittier to enjoy the peace of home life without frequent interruptions. While he acted as one of the secretaries of the National Anti-Slavery Society, he used to be summoned at times to cities where his presence and help were needed in the work. Thus, in 1837 he was for three months in New York. After his return home he was soon called to Philadelphia, where five years before he had helped to form the National Association. To edit an anti-slavery paper called the *Pennsylvania Freeman* now became his business. Happily, his old friends, Mr. and Mrs. Thayer of Haverhill, had, meanwhile, settled in Philadelphia, and they gladly made a home for him with them during his stay in the city. Now must be told what happened to him during his second visit there.

Well did Greenleaf remember his first experience of Philadelphia and all the details connected with it—the arrival at the farm on the misty autumn evening of the messenger from Mr. Garrison—his own journey two or three days later with the other delegates to the unknown town, where no resident could be found willing to take the chair at the convention or in any way support the delegates in the risks they ran. He recalled the solemn scene when all who were present at the meeting signed the "Declaration of Principles" which bound them to help in the cause of freedom, while the groans and hootings of the noisy crowd went on outside.

Since then, what a change had taken place! It was as though a tiny seed sown in the dark, cold earth had grown up into a strong young tree. A number of resolute, hardworking Abolitionists were settled in Philadelphia now, and a building in course of erection in one of the chief streets gave token of the thoughts and aims that were astir among them. This building promised to be the largest and finest in the city. One room in it was to be the office of the *Freeman*, in another the papers and books published by the Association for sale were to be kept. Best of all, its large hall, which would hold two thousand persons, was meant for the use of those who wished to discuss the principles of liberty, the evils of slavery, and the equality of civil rights. There had hitherto been no public room in Philadelphia where such subjects could be discussed.

Greenleaf watched the progress of the stately building with the greatest interest. At last, the workmen were putting the finishing touches to it, and along the front shone out in large gilded letters the name "Pennsylvania Hall." His own newspaper office was ready for use; the book room was filled with stores; and on the 15th of May, 1838, an anti-slavery convention began, which was to last three days, and was looked upon as the opening festival.

The first day's proceedings passed peacefully. Next morning, a meeting of the Women's Anti-Slavery Society was held. Ground floor and galleries were crowded. It was soon very certain that the meeting was composed of foes as well as friends. As the proceedings went on, hisses were to be heard, and angry shouts were raised. Then stones were flung through the windows. It is said that the quiet dignity of the women, who formed so large a party of the assembly, awed the rioters. That day no outbreak took place in the hall. The excited roughs even ceased their cries to listen to the quiet words of a young Quakeress, who spoke in public for the first time. Rising from her seat, she said: "It is not the crashing of these windows nor the maddening rush of these voices that calls me before you. But it is the still, small voice within which may not be withstood that bids me open my mouth for the dumb, that bids me plead the cause of God's perishing poor."

Angelina Grimke Welde was the name of this brave young

Quaker lady. She continued to speak for more than an hour on the sin of slavery, and it is said that the power of her quiet influence was so great that the disturbance inside the hall ceased while her address went on, though the stones flung from the street continued to crash against the windows.

Some germs of right feeling were lying hidden away in the hearts of the unruly mob gathered outside; for when this meeting broke up, both speakers and listeners were allowed to pass out unharmed to their homes. It was in the power of the mayor and chief citizens, if they had chosen to do so, to influence public opinion so that there could have been no repetition of such shameful scenes. But, alas! On the evening of the third day, placards appeared on the city walls encouraging another outbreak, and a great crowd of rioters assembled outside the hall.

The doors were forced open. Books and papers were placed in piles and set on fire. The flames rose up against the dark night sky, while the mob shrieked with excitement. Greenleaf Whittier tried hard to save his office from being sacked. He faced the rabble and addressed them, but to save his life he had to creep through the coalhole and was pelted as he passed along the street. Firemen poured water on the neighboring buildings; but beautiful Pennsylvania Hall was left to its fate, and in a few hours only blackened walls remained.

That night license and disorder triumphed. The mob pressed on to attack some private houses and an institution for black orphans. But the spirit of the lovers of freedom was not cowed. Next day they held a meeting in front of the smoking ruins of Pennsylvania Hall. It must have been a strange sight. Crowds gathered round watching their proceedings. Perhaps they were shamed into silence, for no interruption was made even when a resolution was passed by the meeting to withhold votes from any candidate for Congress who would not bind himself to "discountenance mob-law in its attempts to put down the freedom of speech and press."

Weeks passed, and for the brave little company of anti-slavery workers in Philadelphia there was still constant anxiety, though, for the present, mob rule was at an end, and the city was restored to peace and tranquility. At any time, the slightest pretext might serve as an excuse for a fresh outburst of popular violence, and a very real danger for such a pretext lay always at hand.

For Philadelphia lay on the borders of the Free State of Pennsylvania, while South and West, near at hand, lay the Slave States; and at times a terrified slave fleeing for his life from hunters who were on his track made his way to Philadelphia, hoping to find friends and liberty in the city where all men were free.

Needless to say, there was no safety there for runaway slaves; and Greenleaf Whittier and like-minded men were always on the watch to receive and hide a fugitive, and send him on his way to Canada or some safe refuge in the Northern States. Thus, at one time, a black woman and her children reached Philadelphia in safety at midnight. By some means their flight had been made known to these ever-ready helpers in Philadelphia, who were ready with food and changes of clothes, wigs, and other disguises and help for their further journey.

There was constant excitement in such a life as this, and the experiences in the riot when Pennsylvania Hall was destroyed had already done so much harm to Greenleaf's health, which was never strong, that his friends began to be alarmed about him. His sister Lizzie came to stay with him. Then a physician was called in, who discovered serious trouble with his heart and forbade him any longer to carry on the anxious life he was leading as editor of the *Pennsylvania Freeman*. Still, he clung to his post and disregarded all entreaties till increasing pain and weakness compelled him to give way, and very reluctantly he wrote his editorial farewell for the paper.

CHAPTER 8

LUCY LARCOM

Now, we must picture our poet settled with his family, for a time, to their great joy, in the cottage at Amesbury. His sister's delight was unbounded. "It never feels like home," she wrote to a friend, "when Greenleaf is away," and she devoted herself to him as his nurse and companion. He was very ill, and recovery was slow. Indeed, he never regained any measure of good health from this time, but suffered all the rest of his life from severe headaches and attacks of weakness.

People who live for great causes and to do noble work in the world grow brave and unselfish. It mattered little to Greenleaf Whittier for himself if he felt the pinch of poverty and had hard work to keep his little household free from debt. But it troubled him often, and for years to come, that he could not get luxuries or even ordinary comforts for his dear ones. It was a difficult matter to make even a poor living. His health was broken, and he was no longer equal to any great exertion; and as regards his work as an author, though his name was known all over the States, and his poems were widely read, he was an Abolitionist, and none of his writings could, therefore, be a source of income to him. Yet, notwithstanding pain and weakness, he was constantly at work with his pen.

Visitors often came to the cottage. In the garden room, many of the foremost literary men of the time, both of America and England, sat and talked with the Quaker poet whom they had traveled far to see. Poets, philanthropists, and statesmen made pilgrimage thither, sailing up the Merrimack to the little country town to ask advice from him, and to see the writer of the "Songs of Freedom" that were ringing through the land.

Greenleaf Whittier, with his wide influence, had no difficulty in inducing anti-slavery lecturers to come to little Amesbury to give addresses. Though he was too ill to be present at their meetings, they stayed at his house. It had always been a pleasure to the Whittier family to show hospitality to strangers. It was as much so now as it had been in the days when the old farmhouse door was cheerfully opened to every passerby who needed rest and food. But now visitors could not fail to see the strict economy of the household and to discover that Greenleaf was a very poor man.

One of those visitors was a well-known "Friend" from England named Joseph Sturge. He had worked for years in the same great cause to which Whittier had devoted his powers and had guessed the sacrifices he had made. He was deeply grieved now to notice that many needed comforts were lacking in the invalid poet's house. Before he sailed for England, he left in the hands of a mutual friend a large sum of money, praying Whittier for the sake of their old friendship to use the gift in taking a journey to a warmer climate for the benefit of his health, or in any way that best suited his wishes. Greenleaf used the money for anti-slavery purposes, with warm thanks to his English friend. In his most pressing straits, his thoughts were constantly turning to the needy people he knew and devising means of help and ways of relief for them.

The people of Amesbury were very proud of the poet who had settled in their midst, for they knew well how wide his fame had spread. Better still, he soon became very dear to their simple hearts. He was neither an eloquent man nor a great talker. He never quoted his own poems to his unlearned neighbors. It was his habit to make friends of the poorest among them, and he had a wonderful power of discovering in the most uncouth and apparently stupid if there was any quality in them worthy of respect. On his way to the post office in the evenings he used to go into the general store, where it was the custom of the villagers to meet together; and there, seated on a barrel, he would talk with them of matters that interested them, or touched their daily lives; or discuss politics with the men who crowded round him, and confer with them on the latest news that had reached Amesbury from the busy world. His listeners, unknown to themselves, often carried away from this intercourse some higher thought and nobler aim than they had known before.

The following anecdote gives an instance of the ready way in which he could enter into interest and modes of life which were quite different from his own:

An old farmer—not an Amesbury man—speaking of the poet whom he had once had the privilege of seeing, said (and his words were meant to convey the highest praise):

"He's just as natural and like folks as he can be. He wrote some poems right out here on a board he picked up, and he was sitting in a kitchen chair he had brought out. His poems we can understand. He's like folks—Whittier is."

It is easy to believe that it was a great trial for one who was so eager to help with the work that needed doing in the world, as was Greenleaf Whittier, to lead the inactive life of an invalid. A short poem called "The Waiting," which was written by him about this time, tells us how he longed for strength to help in the struggle for freedom as he had been used to do.

THE WAITING

I wait and watch; before my eyes
Methinks the night grows thin and gray;
I wait and watch the eastern skies,
To see the golden spears uprise
Beneath the oriflamme of day.

Like one whose limbs are bound in trance,
I hear the day sounds swell and grow;
And see across the twilight glance,
Troop after troop, in swift advance,
The shining ones with plumes of snow.

I know the errand of their feet,
I know what mighty work is theirs;
I can but lift up hands unmeet,
The threshing-floors of God to beat,
And speed them with unworthy prayers.

I will not dream in vain despair
The steps of progress wait for me;
The puny leverage of a hair
The planet's impulse well may spare,
A drop of dew the tided sea.

The loss, if loss there be, is mine,
And yet not mine if understood;
For one shall grasp and one resign,
One drink life's rue, and one its wine,
And God shall make the balance good.

O power to do! O baffled will!
O prayer and action! Ye are one.
Who may not strive, may yet fulfill
The harder task of standing still,
And good but wished with God is done!

Greenleaf's sister Lizzie, very different from her quiet brother, attracted people by her brightness and sparkling fun. Some young girls in Amesbury gladly accepted her invitation to begin a reading circle, and each week a little company of village students met at the cottage to talk over books that were chosen for discussion. Greenleaf, interested in all his young sister's plans, used to help to make these meetings successful. Many of the young people who met together in this way owed much in their afterlife to his encouragement and advice.

Time passed. Greenleaf's health improved a little, and in the year 1844, there came a break of six months in this quiet home life. He was invited to edit a paper on the side of liberty in the rising town of Lowell, a few miles from Amesbury, and accepted the post, glad both of a fresh chance for usefulness and of the salary he was to receive.

Lowell was built on the bank of the Merrimack. This river, which flows through meadows at Haverhill and past woods at Amesbury, falls in cascades at a point on its course between the two places. Just there, some great mills were built whose wheels the river turned, and a busy town grew up.

One might fancy that a poet would shun noisy machinery and wander up the riverbank into the peaceful country. On the contrary, our poet was often attracted to the mills, as were also many strangers who used to come long distances to see and talk with the hardworking mill girls who made Lowell famous. The reason for this must now be told.

Perhaps readers of this story know the name of Lucy Larcom, the American poetess, and have read some of her beautiful verses which are so well-known in her native land. To tell the story of Lucy Larcom is to tell why the Lowell mills became famous, and it is to tell the history of one who became in later days one of the dearest friends of Greenleaf and Elizabeth Whittier.

Lucy's happy childhood was passed in the country, "amid the clover blossoms and the songs of birds." She tells us, in the story of her life, how the empty garret in her father's house was like a fairy palace to her, where she hoarded the stray poems she cut out of newspapers and wrote her own little verses, as happy when the rain made music on the roof as when the sunshine poured in through the window. But at ten years old, on the death of her father, she seemed to lose all the poetry and beauty out of her life. For the family removed to Lowell; and even Lucy, small as she was, was sent to one of the mills to earn money by changing bobbins on the frames. For the future, she must spend twelve hours a day amid whirring, flying wheels and spindles, in company with girls who seemed to have no desire to grow up anything better than mindless drudges. This companionship became more painful and distasteful as she began to leave childhood behind her. But what happened? Lucy and her elder sister Emilie had beautiful thoughts and high ideals, which they treasured, notwithstanding their dull, commonplace surroundings. They imparted them to their companions and by the wonderful power of personal influence, became their helpers and leaders to a rich, happy life that had at first seemed impossible.

Just one little seed was sown at first. They persuaded two or three of their fellow workers to try to discover for themselves if it was a fact that "books brought pleasure and interest into life." They lent to one another the few precious volumes they owned, and meetings were arranged to be held, after work was over, at Mrs. Larcom's house, where they talked together over what they had read, and enjoyed comparing favorite passages.

This new influence spread among the mill hands, and the little reading circle was enlarged again and again. The young students borrowed books from the town library. They began to enjoy writing down their thoughts; and, in course of time, they set on foot a magazine, to which one, perhaps, sent a short story, another a poem, in each case the contributor's own composition; while others who were less daring provided some thoughts about the books they happened to be reading. A new tone was thus given to the monotonous daily lives of the mill girls. Their long working hours were brightened, as they almost mechanically tended their machines, by interesting thoughts and memories of what they had read. Lucy had said, and all the girls began to find it was quite true, that "the incessant discord around her could not drown the music of her thoughts if she let them fly high enough," and, like her, they almost ceased to notice the perpetual whirr of the wheels and pulleys.

When Greenleaf Whittier came to Lowell, the "improvement circles" were flourishing. Free lectures had been established for the mill girls who were so eager to gain knowledge, and their magazine, bearing the title of the *Lowell Offering*, was regularly printed and published and found many readers outside the manufacturing town. No wonder was it that Greenleaf, remembering his own struggles in youth, was deeply interested in these wide-minded, hardworking young girls, and especially in Lucy Larcom. His letters interested his mother and sister in her, so that they wanted greatly to see one who had made so much of her opportunities and been such a wise helper and leader to her companions.

And here we will look on into the future and learn something of the kind of life that opened out before Lucy Larcom. Soon after Greenleaf Whittier's stay at Lowell, a chance came for her to enter a training college for women. To pay for her education, she gladly enrolled herself, as poor students were sometimes permitted to do, among the house servants in the college and worked hard with both brain and hands. In a few years, she graduated and came back to Massachusetts, where she not only taught pupils but led a busy literary life. Then she renewed her friendship with the Whittier family, which had been already formed by letters, and there was no more welcome visitor at the cottage than herself.

When his engagement at Lowell was ended, Greenleaf went back to Amesbury. History was making quickly in the United States, in those years before the war broke out—years in which the struggle against slavery was constantly growing stronger. Those were the years in which the course of our story now lies. Terrible deeds of cruelty and wrong kept taking place on the free soil of the North. Fugitive slaves were tracked to Northern cities, hunted out of their hiding places, and dragged back to bondage. Indignant protests were raised in vain. In Congress, shameful compromises were made, Northern senators yielding to the demands of the representatives from the slave-holding states, and the slave power gradually grew stronger and extended its boundaries. On the other side, great numbers of earnest workers were joining the party of the Friends of Freedom; and a mighty wave of influence, spreading over the land from North to South and East to West and rousing men to take part in the struggle against slavery, can be traced to the writings of the poet, who was living in poverty and broken health in a little cottage in a remote country town. If we read, for example, the poem called "Massachusetts to Virginia," and picture to ourselves the event which called it forth, we can understand something of the excitement and enthusiasm which the "Songs of Freedom" produced when they were read at any of the great public anti-slavery meetings which were becoming so frequent throughout the Northern States.

Some years after our poet's death, an American literary man, who was old enough to recall many memories of those exciting times, sent a message to the superintendent of a large school. "Tell your boys and girls," said he, "however much they love and admire Whittier, they cannot know what a fire and passion of enthusiasm he kindled in the hearts of the little company of anti-slavery boys and girls of my time when they read his anti-slavery poems." It was not only grown men and women who were roused by his burning words to take the side of right and justice; his influence also touched the consciences of the youths and maidens of the land. Children learned his poems by heart and recited them at their school festivals, and the aim grew up within them to be brave and true and to lead earnest, real lives.

Colonel Higginson, a well-known American author who did brave deeds for his country in his early manhood, tells us, in the history of his life, how soon after Whittier's poem entitled "Massachusetts to Virginia" appeared in *The Liberator* and was copied into other papers, he, a shy, awkward youth, saw the poet one morning, sitting in a public room in Boston, and longed to give some expression to the enthusiasm he felt both for him and his writings. All he ventured to do, however, was to go to him as he rose to leave the room, and say, "I should like to shake hands with the author of 'Massachusetts to Virginia.'"

Mr. Whittier was always attracted to young people and gave the boy his hand, saying with a kind smile, "Thy name, friend?" Colonel Higginson records, "To me it was like touching a hero's shield. The privilege of Whittier's friendship has been one of the great privileges of my life, but I never forgot that first meeting."

Here is part of a poem which Colonel Higginson wrote later in life to tell something of what he felt he owed to the poet's influence on him in his youth.

At dawn of manhood came a voice to me
That said to startled conscience, sleep no more!

* * * *

If any good to me or from me came
Through life, and if no influence less divine
Has quite usurped the place of duty's flame:
If aught rose worthy in this heart of mine,
Aught that viewed backward, wears no sense of shame:
Bless thee, old friend, for that high call was thine.

Soon after his return from Lowell, Whittier began to write for a new magazine called the *National Era*. The post of corresponding editor was given to him, and then he found fresh ways of helping the young people in whom he took so deep an interest. He made room in the pages of this magazine for the poems of writers who were unknown and friendless and brought them in to notice in this way, helping them constantly by his friendly criticisms and encouragement.

CHAPTER 9

VICTORY WON

To the west of the United States, and adjoining the slave state of Missouri, lay the vast unpeopled territory of Kansas. For more than thirty years, a law known as the Missouri Compromise had forbidden the extension of slavery north or west of Missouri. Now, in the year 1854, this law was repealed, and a new measure was passed by Congress which decreed that the votes of the future dwellers in Kansas should decide whether slavery should, or should not, be established.

This was the signal for a great outcry in the North. The passing of this new law was looked upon as a fresh instance of the plotting for increased power on the part of the Southern senators, and as another proof of the weak yielding of Congress to their demands. The Friends of Freedom resolved to send forth from the Northern states, as settlers in Kansas, farmers and laborers who hated slavery and would therefore vote, when the time came, against admitting slave labor into Kansas.

See what happened. Four or five thousand sturdy, resolute men declared themselves ready to go and make new homes in that unknown land. They would clear the ground and build themselves farms and villages and make a stand for freedom. When the first band of emigrants set forth from Boston, huge crowds of well-wishers assembled to speed them on their way. Loud cheers rent the air. Old neighbors and friends said goodbye to the departing colonists, and many touching farewells were to be seen. At last, strong voices began to sing the "Kansas Emigrants'

Song," which Whittier had written for the occasion, and at the end of every verse a multitude of voices took up the chorus, and so the adventurers were sent forth on their way.

The following is the brave song the poet sent them, and one can well fancy that the hearts of the people, as they sang, would grow warm for liberty.

We cross the prairie as of old
The pilgrims crossed the sea,
To make the West, as they the East,
The homestead of the free.

CHORUS
The homestead of the free, my boys,
The homestead of the free!
To make the West as they the East
The homestead of the free!

We go to rear a wall of men
On freedom's Southern line,
And plant beside the cotton tree
The rugged Northern pine.

(CHORUS)

We're flowing from our native hills
As our free rivers flow:
The blessing of our mother-land
Is on us as we go.

(CHORUS)

We go to plant her common schools
On distant prairie swells,
And give the Sabbaths of the wild
The music of her bells.

(CHORUS)

Upbearing like the ark of old
The Bible in our van,
We go to test the truth of God
Against the fraud of man.

(CHORUS)

We'll tread the prairie as of old
Our fathers sailed the sea,
And make the West, as they the East
The homestead of the free!

(CHORUS)

Time passed, and more bands of emigrants followed the first little company to Kansas. Villages and farms grew up. But, terrible to tell, border ruffians from the South fell upon the settlements and burned the houses, destroyed the crops, and killed numbers of the people, hoping thus to drive away the men who were resolved that Kansas should not form another slave state. This led to a kind of civil war, for the Northern states sent troops to Kansas to defend the settlers.

Our poet wrote for the Kansas emigrants a second and very different poem from the first he had sent them. It was, in truth, a dirge called "Le Marais du Cygne," from the name of the spot where the massacre took place. Here is one of the verses:

Strong man of the prairies
Mourn bitter and wild!
Wail, desolate woman!
Weep, fatherless child!
But the grain of God springs up
From ashes beneath,
And the crown of His harvest
Is life out of death.

The last lines tell just what sort of consoling thoughts were filling Greenleaf Whittier's mind at this time. A terrible struggle was going on in his native land, and worse was plainly still to come. But as he watched the progress of the cause of liberty, he felt sure of triumph in the long run. There is a great power at work in every nation, which we call "public opinion." This fact everyone is ready to acknowledge. Not so clearly do we always see the wonderful influence which even a handful of right-minded, resolute people exercise over public opinion. The merchants, lawyers, and clergy in the Northern states were the last to forsake the pro-slavery party, yet the great mass of the people were gradually growing stronger in their opposition to slavery, and this was, in some measure, due to the fact that many of the chief writers were following Whittier's example and coming out strongly on the side of freedom. In 1857, a magazine called the *Atlantic Monthly* was set on foot; and to this paper not only Greenleaf Whittier but others of the foremost American authors—Lowell, Longfellow, Mrs. Beecher Stowe, Oliver Wendell Holmes, and more, sent poems and papers on all the leading questions of the day that needed reformation, and among them, of course, slavery held a foremost place. Good men and women are God's tools by which He mends the world. Happily, His faithful workers were busy in the foremost ranks and also in the unnoticed, common ways of life; and none of the seeds they sowed would be wasted.

Whittier believed greatly in the power of quiet, unseen influence, and some of his poems were written to encourage solitary, unnoticed laborers.

In the year 1858, Mrs. Whittier died. The loss of their mother was a deep grief to the brother and sister. They were now left together in the cottage. Aunt Mercy had passed away two years before.

"I have been sitting by the bedside of my dear mother during the last few weeks," wrote Greenleaf to a friend, "following her in love and sympathy to the very entrance of the valley of shadows. She is no longer with us. The end was one of exceeding peace, a quiet and beautiful dismissal. The world looks far less than it did when she was with us. Half the motive power of life is lost."

In this great sorrow, his thoughts turned back to the old home they had left twenty years before; and in a poem called "Telling the Bees," he described, with tender touches, things that had been so dear to him there in his boyhood, and which were associated with his mother's memory—the path over Job's Hill, the stepping stones in the brook, the beehives that stood in a row in the garden, the roses at his mother's window, and the evening light that used to shine on the old farmhouse and make it beautiful.

About this time, he wrote some verses called "The Garden," to be sung at a harvest fair in Amesbury. They were afterwards translated into Portuguese and read at a harvest festival in Portugal, and into Italian and sung by Italian peasants as they gathered in the grapes. One day, a friend told him how two ragged laboring men, who looked as if no poetry ever entered into their sordid lives, were seen to stand before the window of a poor shop in a little, narrow street in Boston, where these verses were displayed, spelling them out carefully as if the unwonted ideas gave them pleasure. This was good news for the poet, for he loved to minister by his words to the toiling and heavily laden people and to open their eyes to see the beauty in the world.

Now, our story takes us again into stormy times. A great event was at hand—the election of a new president for the United States. People in all parts of the land, both North and South, were in the wildest excitement. For this reason—it would be in the power of the new president to decree whether fresh slave states should be formed and added to the Union.

On March 4, 1861, Abraham Lincoln entered office. Straightway, the decree went forth that slavery should not advance further on the free lands of the North and West. On this, a rebellion broke out in the Southern states. A convention was summoned at Charleston in South Carolina, at which it was resolved that the Southern states should break away from the Union. The first shot in the civil war that followed was fired from Fort Sumter in Charleston Harbor. Up rose the people of the North to defend the Union and suppress the rebellion, and like a fierce storm or a raging fire, the war spirit swept over the land.

Now, Whittier had been a lover of peace all his life, as had his Quaker ancestors before him, and the breaking out of this war was a deep grief to him. For four long years it lasted, and relatives and old neighbors and friends who took opposite sides in the conflict met on the battlefields and shot each other down. Yet he was the people's poet and could not be silent in this great crisis of the national life. During the war his poems were heard in every marching column, and President Lincoln said of them, "They are just the kind of songs I want the soldiers to hear." Some of them were set to music and sung in the Union camps. On one occasion, a message was sent to the Quaker poet from some of the regiments in the Union army, begging him to come and visit the men in their encampment. "Your verses have made us all your friends," they sent word, "lightening the wearisomeness of our march and brightening our lonely campfires."

What sort of verses could this peace-lover write, which people, whose hearts were centered on the soldiers and the battlefield, would ever care to read? We may be sure he never wrote in praise of the pomp of war, nor tried to glorify the slaughter on the battle-fields. This was all horrible in his eyes. If it was a necessity, to him it was a sad necessity. He could see no bright side to the resort to arms. But this he could and did do. He could keep before men's minds the thought of the greatness of the cause about which they went to war, could make them eager to gain liberty for the slaves, and be brave to defend the right and put an end to injustice and oppression.

The following are some of his war verses addressed to men of the state of Massachusetts:

Shrink not from strife unequal,
With the best is always hope,
And ever in the sequel
God holds the right side up.

✳ ✳ ✳ ✳

Fling abroad the scrolls of Freedom!
Speed them onward far and fast!
O'er hill and valley speed them
Like the sibyl's on the blast.

✳ ✳ ✳ ✳

On they come,—the free battalions!
East, and West, and North they come,
And the heartbeat of the millions
Is the beat of Freedom's drum.
"To the tyrants' plot no favor!
No heed to place fed knaves!
Bar and bolt the door forever
Against the land of slaves!"
Hear it mother Earth, and hear it

The Heavens above us spread!
The land is raised—its spirit
Was sleeping but not dead!

Whittier loved and honored every brave soul that stood firm to the right, but he never found his heroes in men simply because they were bold in battle and valiant under fire when their blood was hot.

On one occasion during the war, the Southern army, under General Jackson, marched into a Northern town and took possession. Every house and shop was shut, and all the Union flags, the signal of freedom, were taken down and hidden away. But as the rebel army marched up the street with the famous general at its head, an old woman of ninety-six years of age, named Barbara Frietchie, opened her window and held out the Union flag.

The order to halt was given, and the soldiers stood still. "Fire!" was the next command, and the banner hung drooping from its staff. Barbara stretched out her arm from the window as far as she could and waved the flag over the soldiers' heads, crying, "Fire at this old gray head, boys! It is not more venerable than your flag!" The story tells us that the general gave orders to his troops to march on, and they "passed in silence with downcast looks." The brave old lady fastened the loyal banner, and it waved there all through the time that the rebel army occupied the town. Barbara Frietchie's deed Mr. Whittier took as the subject for a ballad. It was an instance of the kind of courage he held dear, the courage which helps people to stand firm to principle.

Those years during which the war lasted were full of pain and anxiety for the lovers of their country. Still one hope ever shone brightly before our poet and his friends and fellow workers, and they toiled on that they might help to make this hope a reality. This was the hope that through the hateful agency of war, their native land might be redeemed from the sin and curse of slavery.

Truly it was a "red-letter day" when, at last, a law was passed by Congress abolishing slavery forever from the United States. That day, Greenleaf Whittier was sitting in the Quaker Meeting House at Amesbury, where the few "Friends" who lived in the neighborhood had gathered for worship in the middle of the week, according to their custom. He was giving thanks in silence, for he knew that the passing of this "constitutional amendment" was close at hand, when suddenly, the roar of cannon and the ringing of bells broke upon the quiet of the place, and he knew that the work which he had given the best years of his life to bring about was done.

Straightway, a grand song of praise arose within him, and when he came home, he repeated two verses of it to his friends, who were awaiting his return in the garden room. This poem he called "Laus Deo," and speaking of it afterwards to his friend Lucy Larcom, he said, "It sang itself while the bells rang."

It is done!
Clang of bell and roar of gun,
Send the tidings up and down.
How the belfries rock and reel!
How the great guns, peal on peal,
Fling the joy from town to town!

* * * *

Ring and swing,
Bells of joy! on morning's wing
Send this song of praise abroad!
With a sound of broken chains
Tell the nations that He reigns,
Who alone is Lord and God.

CHAPTER 10

AFTER THE WAR

In the memorable year 1865, when the war came to an end in the United States, Greenleaf Whittier was not far from sixty years of age. There was no longer any need for him to bend all his energies in a struggle against a great wrong. That year it must have seemed to him as if he turned over a new page in the book of his life. For not only was the work over, to which he had devoted himself for so long; at the same time, the sunlight passed away from his home. His dear companion, his sister Elizabeth, after three months' painful illness, was dead.

Soon after her death, he wrote thus to Miss Larcom: "We were friends before thee knew my dear sister; but now all who loved her seem nearer and dearer to me. I feel it difficult even now to realize all I have lost, but I sorrow without repining, and with a feeling of submission to the Will which I am sure is best. If I can help it, I do not intend the old homestead be gloomy and forbidding through any selfish regrets. She would not have it so. She would have it cheerful, with the old familiar faces of the friends whom she loved and still loves."

The first poem he wrote after he lost his sister was called "The Vanishers." It was this poem that Lucy Larcom, who had been Elizabeth's dearest friend, read in the old farmhouse at Haverhill when, some years later after Mr. Whittier's death, a service was held there in his memory.

Here are some of the verses:

THE VANISHERS

Sweetest of all child-like dreams
In the simple Indian lore,
Still to me the legend seems
Of the shapes who flit before.

Flitting, passing, seen and gone,
Never reached nor found at rest,
Baffling search, but beckoning on
To the sunset of the Blest.

* * * *

Doubt who may, O friend of mine!
Thou and I have seen them too:
On before with beck and sign
Still they glide, and we pursue.

Glimpses of immortal youth,
Gleams and glories seen and flown,
Far-heard voices sweet with truth,
Airs from viewless Eden blown,—

Beauty that eludes our grasp,
Sweetness that transcends our taste,
Loving hands we may not clasp,
Shining feet that mock our haste—

Gentle eyes we closed below,
Tender voices heard once more,
Smile and call us, as they go
On and onward, still before.

Guided thus, O friend of mine!
Let us walk our little way,
Knowing by each beckoning sign
That we are not quite astray.

Chase we still, with baffled feet,
Smiling eye and waving hand,
Sought and seeker soon shall meet,
Lost and found, in Sunset Land!

The people of Amesbury, who loved and honored their poet friend, mourned over his loss and showed him their sympathy in many touching ways. By and by he began to take interest in the building of a new schoolhouse in Amesbury and to work in his garden as he had been used to do. To wander in the woods seemed to soothe his sorrow, and he found comfort in visiting Haverhill, where the river banks were in full beauty.

Before the summer was over, the lonely garden room held a great treasure—a beautiful portrait of Elizabeth, sent by Lucy Larcom. It was hung on the wall opposite the portrait of his mother, and in course of time, these two faces looking down upon him, Greenleaf wrote the long poem "Snowbound," in which he tells the story of the old home at Haverhill and describes in tender words the dear ones of the family, so many of whom were gathered to their rest.

"Snowbound" was published with a picture of the farmhouse in a snowstorm as frontispiece. The sale of the book brought him a large sum of money. His first thought when he found how his circumstances had changed was a sad one. Those for whom he had so longed to buy comforts and luxuries were gone!

And now, suddenly, the contest about slavery being at an end, Whittier found himself a popular poet. But he did not like to hear the word "famous" applied to himself. "I have never thought of

myself," he said, "as a poet, in the sense in which we use the word
when we speak of great poets. I have just said, from time to time,
the things I had to say, and it has been a series of surprises to me
that people should remember them so long."

To no one except himself, however, was it a matter of surprise
that he had won fame. For years past, whenever there was a cause,
"some burning lyric of his had flown over the country to warn
and rally." Before the end of the war, he had written, besides prose
works, three hundred poems, of which more than one-third were
on the subject of slavery. There was now no longer any need for
him to send his songs of freedom ringing through the land; but
his work as a poet was not done. We shall see in a little while by
what sort of poems he went on helping the world. But first we
must picture him in the changed life which began for him after the
death of his sister.

It was very natural that his friends should now regret that the
lonely poet had never married. Those who knew him best were
aware that the care of his mother and sister had prevented him
from forming other ties. So great had been his love for them that
he never sorrowed over this when on their death he was left alone,
and they were cheerful words he wrote one day to a friend in reply
to sympathy on this point—

"My life has been, on the whole, quite as happy as I deserved
or had a right to expect. I know there has been something very
sweet and beautiful missed, but I have no reason to complain. I
have learned, at last, to look into happiness with the eyes of others,
and to thank God for the happy unions and holy firesides I have
known."

Self came always last with Greenleaf Whittier. The happiness of
his life lay in loving and helping his fellow man. A very few words
will make for us a new picture of the poet at this time and show
how his days went on.

A niece came to keep house for him. Though much of each

day he was in pain, and though there were so many vacant places around his hearth, there was never any sign of gloom about him. In the garden room, visitors were welcomed as they had always been—both old friends and new admirers who came from far and wide to see the author of "Snowbound," which had taken the land, as it were, by storm. Greenleaf Whittier's large heart was ready to welcome all who came to him. Here are two stories in illustration.

One day a young man carrying a pack came to the cottage door. He was a peddler selling his wares as he went from village to village, in hope of earning money enough to pay his college fees. He was asked, and told his history. He knew of no lodging for the night. The cottage was full, for the "Friends" were just then holding their "Quarterly Meeting" at Amesbury; but Mr. Whittier took the traveler to a neighbor's house and gained the promise of a night's rest for him. This was the kind of youth the poet always wanted to help. His sympathies went out to him. Perhaps he wished to be certain that the stranger was kindly treated and encouraged; for in the evening he went to bring the youth back to his own house, where he would give up his own bed and sleep on a sofa himself. This was not permitted, but next morning, Whittier came to his neighbor's house to extend kindness, and asked the peddler if he would like to go with him to the meetings he was to attend that day, seated him there next to himself, and sent the youth again on his way with a fresh fund of hope and courage with him.

An old washerwoman in Amesbury, one of his many friends, had saved enough money by her hard work to buy a little home for her old age and her children's future dwelling. There must be a celebration of such an event, said the poet, and he came among his poor neighbors to the little feast, and read a poem which he had written for the occasion.

Numbers of similar stories might be told showing how, by his overflowing kindness and readiness to help, he won the love of all with whom he came in contact, and this affection was more precious to him than was the fame which, as we have seen, also fell to his lot. Dumb creatures always found a friend in him, and all his life it was his habit to make pets of birds and dogs. For a long time, he had one special favorite in a gray parrot that sat on the back of his chair at mealtimes. When the bird died, his master wrote thus to Miss Larcom:

"I have met with a real loss; poor Charlie is dead. He has gone where the good parrots go. He has been ailing and silent for some time, and he finally died. Don't laugh at me, but I am sorry enough to cry if it would do any good. He was an old friend. Dear Lizzie liked him, and he was the heartiest, jolliest, pleasantest old fellow I ever saw. And speaking of this reminds me of a little verse I have by me, suggested by one of his sayings. I enclose it. Perhaps it might help a corner in *Our Young Folks*.

Our Young Folks was the name of a magazine for children which Lucy Larcom edited, and there the poem in memory of the gray parrot appeared under the title of "The Common Question," to the delight of doubtless hosts of boys and girls in America, to whom Mr. Whittier's name was familiar as a household word.

THE COMMON QUESTION

Behind us at our evening meal
The gray bird ate his fill,
Swung downward by a single claw,
And wiped his hooked bill.

He shook his wings and crimson tail,
And set his head aslant,
And in his sharp, impatient way,
Asked, "What does Charlie want?"

"Fie, silly bird," I answered, "tuck
Your head beneath your wing

And go to sleep."—But o'er and o'er
He asked the self same thing.

Then smiling to myself I said,
"How like are men and birds!"
We all are saying what he says
In action or in words.

The boy with ship and top and drum,
The girl with hoop and doll,
And men with lands and houses ask
The question of poor Poll.

However full, with something more
We fain the bag would cram,
We sigh above our crowded nets
For fish that never swam.

The dear God hears and pities all,
He knoweth all our wants,
And what we blindly ask of Him
His love withholds or grants.

And so I sometimes think our prayers
Might well be merged in one,
And next, and perch, and hearth, and church
Repeat, "Thy will be done."

And now, before this chapter ends, a few words must be said
as to the sort of poems he wrote when the "Songs of Freedom"
were no longer needed. They were poems which helped his fellow
man in a different way, but no less powerfully. Numbers of people
in those days, as now, were puzzling over creeds they could not

understand and sorely troubled by doctrines which took away their peace of mind. Greenleaf Whittier had held all his life a very simple faith in the loving Fatherhood of God. Thus, he said, in one of his poems:

"I only know I cannot drift
Beyond His love and care."

And to a friend he once wrote: "All that science and criticism can urge cannot shake the evident truth that God asks me to be true, just, merciful, and loving; and, because He asks me to be so, I know that He is Himself what He requires of me." So his religion was a religion of everyday life, and he made Christ his leader and pattern.

Our friend, our brother, and our Lord,
What may thy service be?
No name, nor form, nor ritual word
But simply following thee.

We bring no ghastly holocaust,
We pile no graven stone,
He serves thee best who loveth most
His brothers and thine own.

We see in these verses the ideas that had acted on his own life and made him the champion of the oppressed slave and ever ready with his help for all who needed it; and such were some of the thoughts which in his poems he now gave to the world.

The poet Oliver Wendell Holmes said of him: "His influence on the religious history of America has been greater than that of any occupant of her pulpits." Thus, fed in spirit, he grew in beauty of character, and as old age drew near, we find him writing:

All the jarring notes of life
Seem blending in a psalm,
And all the angles of its strife
Slow rounding into calm.

And so the shadows fall apart,
And so the west winds play,
And all the windows of my heart
I open to the day.

CHAPTER 11

OAK KNOLL

Not many miles from Amesbury, near an old road that was once the highway between Newburyport and Boston, lies a beautiful estate called Oak Knoll. Mr. Whittier had given this name to the place, which was owned by three ladies—his cousins. They had always held him in most affectionate regard, and when, in the year 1876, his niece married, who had kept his house since the death of his sister, they besought him to make Oak Knoll his home. So from that time he lived there for a part of each year; but he paid frequent and long visits to the cottage at Amesbury for the sake of the dear memories which made every room sacred to him.

Oak Knoll was an old house standing in the midst of extensive grounds. Elms, oaks, chestnuts, and pines made shady avenues and stood singly or in groups over the lawns and on the hill which rose before the house. There were orchards of pear and apple trees; green arches served for gateways into a flower garden close to the dwelling, and in this garden a fountain played.

A library was built especially for the poet's use. It faced the west that he might enjoy the sunset; and from the windows of the room in which he slept, there were fine views of the hill, the flower garden, and the fountain, and of far away meadows and of trees rising up in the distance against the sky.

On fine mornings Mr. Whittier was often to be seen at work in the garden before breakfast. No one was allowed to shoot on the estate, and the birds and squirrels he loved were tame enough to come to the windows to be fed.

It was his habit in the summer, at times, to go with a party of relatives among the hills. He always liked young people to be among the number, and they flocked round him wherever he went. He planned excursions for them, which he thought they would enjoy, and entered into all their interests. He was always ready to talk sociably with strangers whom he met on these journeys; in fact, he went through life with kindly words always on his lips and friendly hands outstretched. Probably no one ever loved nature more, and numbers of his poems, among them "The River Path" and "Seeking the Waterfall," give us word pictures that bring the loveliest scenes before us.

But our poet is growing old—hearing begins to fail, sight grows dimmer, and he suffers more pain. Still, he is always patient and cheerful. On the eve of his seventieth birthday, the literary men of America made ready to celebrate the event. Tributes in prose and verse poured in upon him, and a great banquet was held in his honor in Boston, at which, with much reluctance, the poet was persuaded to be present. As he entered the room, the whole assembly rose and welcomed him with hearty cheers. Longfellow and other celebrities read verses which they had written for the occasion.

One by one his old companions were leaving earth. One of the most valued, William Lloyd Garrison, who had been dear to him from his boyhood, died in the year 1879, and Mr. Whittier's fine poem to his memory was read at the graveside. We can fancy the white-haired poet sometimes musing in the firelight over his past life and living over again in his thoughts the years of struggle in which Garrison and he had fought shoulder to shoulder. "My friends are passing away," he wrote, when he heard of Garrison's death, "and I am old enough to be done with work. I must wait for the fresh, strong life of immortality in the hope I may be enabled to do better with the talents God has given me than I have done."

Sometimes events took place which seemed like links with

the past. They were always welcome. One day, a little company
of black men called at the cottage in Amesbury and asked if they
could see Mr. Whittier. They were a band of singers who had just
come back from a tour in Europe, where they had been earning
money to provide the means of education for the freed blacks in
America. Their visit to Amesbury was like that of pilgrims to a
shrine; for though they had been admitted to sing before emperors
and kings in foreign courts, it seemed to them a greater honor to
enter into the presence of the old man who had done so much to
give freedom to their race. They were received in the garden room
with the usual kindness and sang some of their choicest songs to
Mr. Whittier. At last, they rose to go and ended with a musical
benediction in farewell:

The Lord bless thee and keep thee,
The Lord make His face shine upon thee,
And be gracious unto thee.
The Lord lift up the light of His countenance
Upon thee, and give thee peace.

The voices of the singers trembled with emotion; the old poet
listened with bowed head while the tears ran down his cheeks.
"God bless you all, goodbye," were his parting words as he gave his
hand to each.

On December 17, 1887, from morning till night, Oak Knoll
was crowded with a multitude of distinguished visitors. The poet
was eighty years old. By special train, in carriages, and on foot
came the messengers from "every section in the commonwealth,"
carrying greetings to him. An address bearing many hundreds of
autographs from state officials and senators was presented, and
distinguished citizens from Massachusetts and other states came
out to see him.

"In intervals of the visitations on my birthday," he said

afterwards, "I wondered at my age and if it was possible that I was the little boy on the Haverhill Farm, unknown and knowing nobody beyond my home horizon. I could not quite make the connection between the white-haired man and the black-locked boy. I could not help a feeling of loneliness, thinking of having outlived so many of my life companions, but I was still grateful to God that I had not outlived my love for them and for those still living."

As age advanced he did not cease from writing. When eighty-three years old, he corrected the proof of a new volume of poems, entitled *At Sundown*. His last birthday was kept at Amesbury. In addition to other honors, it was observed as a holiday in the public schools, and many hundreds of young black people sent greetings and presents. In the winter of the year 1891, he had an attack of influenza, of which he felt the effects for many months. The following summer he went for a visit to the home of an old friend at Hampton Falls, only seven miles away from Amesbury, and some relatives were always at hand watching him and caring for him tenderly. For himself, his days were passed in cheerfulness and peace as he waited for the summons to come up higher.

He had not long to wait. Before the autumn was over, a slight stroke of paralysis warned that his end was near. He only lingered three days. His friends were grieved that they could not remove him to the cottage at Amesbury where he had always wished to die, but when they told him this, he answered, "It is all right—everybody is so kind." Now and then a few whispered words assured the watchers that he knew all would be well, and more than once the farewell message fell from his lips, "Love—love to all the world."

On September 6, as the day was breaking, he passed peacefully away, and as the spirit took its flight, one of the little group of mourners gathered round him repeated his poem "At Last."

AT LAST

When in my day of life the night is falling,
And in the winds from unsunned places blown,
I hear far voices out of darkness calling
My feet to paths unknown.

Thou who hast made my home of life so pleasant,
Leave not its tenant when the walls decay!
O Love Divine, O Helper ever present,
Be Thou my strength and stay!

Be near me when all else is drifting,
Earth, sky, home's pictures, days of shade and shine,
And kindly faces to my own uplifting
The love which answers mine.

I have but Thee, my Father! let Thy Spirit
Be with me then to comfort and uphold:
No gate of pearl, no branch of palm I merit,
No street of shining gold.

Suffice it if—my good and ill unreckoned,
And both forgiven through thy abounding grace—
I find myself by hands familiar beckoned
Unto my fitting place.

Some humble door among Thy many mansions,
Some sheltering shade where sin and striving cease,
And flows forever through Heaven's green expansions,
The river of Thy peace.

There, from the music round about me stealing,
I fain would learn the new and holy song,

And find at last, beneath Thy trees of healing
The life for which I long.

As soon as the sad news was known in Haverhill and Amesbury, the bells were tolled, and the flags were hung at half-mast. The lifeless body was carried to the cottage at Amesbury and laid in the garden room, and thousands of people passed silently through the house to take a last look at his face.

The following day, in beautiful September sunshine, the funeral service was held in the garden, where seats for many hundreds were placed on the grass, and hundreds more stood beneath the fruit trees. It was a wonderful uprising of the people to do honor to his memory. Old and young, rich and poor, white people and black, men of renown and barefooted boys were there, gathered together in loving reverence. A few hours later, while the hills were still bathed in golden light, the sad procession passed from the cottage to the "Friends" burial place in the village cemetery. There, in a grave lined with ferns, roses, and goldenrod, they laid the worn-out body to rest. A plain marble tablet marks the spot, and a tall cedar tree stands at the foot. Around are the last resting places of the relatives with whom his boyhood and youth were spent in the old home at Haverhill.

THE END

"Whittier's Birthplace" by Thomas Hill (1829–1908), c. 1865

Portrait of John Greenleaf Whittier at age 29, published by Dodd, Mead and Co, NY, 1898 (based on a painting by Bass Otis)

Photograph of John Greenleaf Whittier c. 1840–1860

Whittier Home in Amesbury, MA by Daderot, CC BY-SA 3.0

Lithograph of John Greenleaf Whittier in 1887